WOW!

Women of Legacy

WOW! Women of Legacy

How To Live A Life Of Legacy

Earma Brown
Pink Tree Publishing
Dallas, Texas

All Scripture quotations are from the King James Version of the New Scofield Bible. 1967 Printed by Oxford University Press. All New Testament definitions are taken from W.E. Vines Dictionary of New Testament Words.

ISBN-10: 09895524-4-6
ISBN-13: 978-0-9895524-4-8

Published in the United States of America.

Early Praise for the WOW! Women Trilogy of Books

Earma, I wanted you to know how much I have been enjoying reading your WOW! Women book. It literally has been like God told you to write it just for me. I can now identify how much I have dealt with rejection in my life. Just the other day, I found myself recognizing the spirit of rejection. I immediately thought of you and your book. I responded with a right response: I repented and forgave the person. Thank you for writing this book… —*Charlette Lakey*

Absolutely!! I would love to bless my entire book club with a copy and we will make it the highlight for our first meeting. We would certainly love for you to join us for the discussion as it really feed my spirit when I read it for the first time. It is truly needed within our club ministry right now so it will be my absolute pleasure… to purchase books…as I will gift the books to them as a stocking stuffer for Christmas. *—Jackie, Girlfriends, Book Club President*

It's a must read because, she taps into your mind: meaning she talks about things that you have questioned yourself about, makes you think about things that you have said or thought and you know that you shouldn't have said or though lol… she helps us to tap into and appreciate who God has made us to be, the book is very enlightening. Thank you Earma :))) —*Kitty*

Thank you for the book. It has given me so much hope. As I sat and read WOW! my mind went back to my life when I first got married and I began to read my Bible and God gave me a new life and now my life could not be better. I wake up in the morning and say Thank you Jesus! —*Love, your Aunt Samella*

I loved the book. I ordered some to give to young ladies so they would be encouraged. I am going to spread the good news to women at my church also…because this book is definitely Good news. —unknown

Earma, you outdid yourself. WOW! is a must read for ALL women. I read it and it was a fantastic book. I can't wait for the next one. You keep empowering women. I can't say enough good things about WOW! I truly loved it. —*Vickye Allison Frazier*

Just stopping by to congratulate you on WOW! books. Excellent book so far. I've been reading Women of Worth since I left Chicago. I plan to finish it tonight (especially luv the chapter on "Unlocking Your Potential." I've already promised to give it to Kesha once I finish it as well as recommend it to other females within my social network. Personally, I think this book should be on Oprah's book of the month. Keep making the family proud with your superb writing and inspirational messages!!!! —*Jacque Morrison*

Thank you for teaching the class "WOW! Women Encouraging Women to Their Purpose and Destiny" We have been hearing good reports of the blessing you were to your students. We appreciate your faithfulness and service to the Lord in teaching His children. We know many have been blessed by your obedience to serve Him. —*Late Melinda Manning, Pastor, Covenant Church, Carrollton, Texas*

Earma, I cannot express enough to you the timeliness of this message! Many, many women will be blessed and grow through this teaching. You are out at the threshold of a great and mighty "new thing" that God is doing for His women who search after His heart!! You are blessed – you are anointed. You are on your way. I considered it a great pleasure that you allowed me the privilege to review your material. —*Darla Knoll, Former Women's Ministry Coordinator, Covenant Church, Carrollton, Texas.*

Dearest Earma, thank you so much for sharing your life, your heart and your wisdom. But especially, thank you for your love! Thank you for building us up. —*Mary, WOW Class attendee.*

I look forward to WOW, Women of Destiny the class. It has been a blessing in my life. Thank you. —*Illya Roberts*

Earma, it has been a blessing to have you as a teacher these last few weeks. We appreciated your sweet spirit! Since you are such a giver we felt led to give you a token of our love for you... —*Jane & Cleo, WOW class attendees.*

I've struggled with so many of the same issues that I was encouraged to see someone bold enough to write about it. I enjoyed the class and I'm looking forward to the books. —*Bettie Cormel, WOW class attendee.*

To add your testimony or positive comment to this list for next book, please visit Earma at http://wowontheweb.com/testimonies/

Dedication

I dedicate this book to my precious husband:

Varn Brown, Sr.

Thank you for your support and encouragement through the years. When I succeeded you cheered and when I missed the mark you rallied in kindness, when I fell short you extended a helping hand and when I am victorious, you can be sure you will help me lead the celebration.

Epigraph

We will not hide these truths from our children; we will tell the next generation about the glorious deeds of the LORD, about his power and his mighty wonders. For he issued his laws to Jacob; he gave his instructions to Israel. He commanded our ancestors to teach them to their children, so the next generation might know them--even the children not yet born--and they in turn will teach their own children. So each generation should set its hope anew on God, not forgetting his glorious miracles and obeying his commands.... —*Psalm 78:4-7*

Acknowledgements

Special thanks to all the women and men that have imparted to my life and to this message. You have helped divide my sorrows, multiply my joys and participated in my victories.

Book Three:

WOW! Women of Legacy

How To Live A Life Of Legacy

A little girl was born in a time of turmoil for Israel. She was an orphan with no future and no destiny. Yet, through the hand of God she was raised to power and destiny. Or so it seemed, what happened next could have turned her bright future to darkness. She and her nation fasted, prayed and acted in the power of God. In the process, she learned a secret about God's Recompense that brought salvation to her nation with an unexpected upset of her enemies' plans so powerful her legacy echoes through the centuries for generations to come.

An Ethiopian Queen and her entourage filed into the court of King Solomon. They came in with respect, bearing an elephantine load of gifts and expecting a return on their investment. What they received surprised a nation and is still heralded today as spectacular. This royal Ethiopian woman acted as an example for women today. Jesus commended her for pursuing and receiving something that many don't value. She received from the best source of that day, wisdom, knowledge, revelation, an education.

Queen Jezebel distinguished herself in creating an evil legacy for Israel. The people trembled at the mention of her name. Under her rule, 850 of the palace prophets were executed in a battle of the gods hosted and led by Prophet Elijah. Her decrees sent the prophets in the land into hiding. What power did she weld that all Christians do well to avoid? Her life and evil actions still symbolize the spirit of control and the sin of rebellion against God today.

Chapter Four: Overcoming The Giants Of Your Generation   81
A Woman's Will To Win

Two women were faced with a hard decision at the crossroads of life. Either way, their destinies would be changed. One chose to go back and the other chose to go forward. They both grew to become notorious matriarchs in the lives of their family and God's chosen people, Israel. Through God's sovereignty the results resound through the centuries to now. What did they use to change their future and the lives of others forever? They used the secret power of choice to pivot their destiny and leave a legacy, like no other.

Chapter Five: Passing The Torch Of Legacy   101
A Woman's Torch Of Life

Lois and Eunice are commended for their personal faith in the New Testament. With God's help, they rose above the rest, in their personal faith and preparing their life as a pattern to pass. What did they do that caught the attention of the Apostle Paul? These two women became famous for raising a godly young man in the midst of an ungodly society. They prepared a torch of legacy for the next generation.

∽

A Woman's Life Well Lived

Her humility brought her before the angel Gabriel sent with a holy message from God. Her response to the angel caused her to receive a 400-year-old prophecy fulfilled. Mary, a virgin gave birth to a child and called his name, Jesus. God's glorious plan of salvation for mankind was consummated through Jesus. What did Mary know that brought her from giving birth to Jesus in a stable to being numbered in the Upper Room on the Day of Pentecost? She used the secret power of a 'yielded vessel' to multiply her future and the destiny of countless.

Preface

Dear Woman of Legacy:

Welcome to the third study in the WOW! Women Series. All three books were written as stand-alone studies. I offer a little of my history and testimony for those of you joining us for the first time. When I began writing the WOW! Women material, I was reaching for women delivered from abusive lifestyles who wanted to rebuild their self-image and life in God.

God burned in my mind one evening before a Bible study I was teaching for a rowdy bunch of maximum security women inmates in the Dallas County Jail, "Tell them they are WOW! Women of Worth..."

After teaching the WOW! Women classes, I discovered another facet of what God wanted to do with this message. Yes, women have been gaining a right image (a biblical perspective) of themselves. But the class sessions and now the books have become a time of women from any background with different struggles coming together as women encouraging one another to victory, destiny and legacy in their lives.

Over twenty years ago, I was a victim of spouse abuse. On the outside, except for being abnormally thin, I looked normal. Yet, on the inside, I was wounded and walking around humped over with my arms hanging to the ground. I used to drive by the city's heavily shaded cemetery not far from my workplace and envy the people lying out there under the trees in peace.

I thought often about giving up thinking, "It must be nice to be in total rest without pretense and no wounds to hide." Yet, something within me would whisper, "Your life is not always going to be like this." I now know that something was someone, the Holy Spirit, keeping a spark of hope alive in me.

My God has been faithful for my life is nothing like it used to be. During that season of my life, I moved as far away as I could get (about 600 miles) from my then hopeless life. The rest is history and a long story; after years of denying me a divorce, the abusive husband, eventually divorced me. I recommitted my life to Jesus, later that same year.

My Lord and I began putting the fragmented pieces of my life together. He began walking me through steps to healing and wholeness. Twenty-four years ago, he rewarded my faith with a caring husband and filled my heart with compassion for His wonderful creation WOMAN.

From this compassion, the message of 'WOW! Women' was birthed. The material was developed from the healing and process it has taken for me to think right about myself, connect with my destiny and build legacy for future generations. God began to develop truth in me that became strategies to becoming the women of victory and destiny He designed for us all to become.

My goal is to bring a message of hope to those who hunger for God's destiny and purpose in their lives. In part one of this series of books, we uncovered a trail of seven biblical truths that show value in a woman's life by helping us answer the four classic questions of life afresh and sometimes for the first time: 'Where did I come from?' Who am I?' "Why am I here?' and just as importantly, 'Where am I going?'

In WOW! Women of Destiny, we continued the biblical trail leading to our passion, purpose and the power to fulfill our destiny. Each chapter was designed to leave every woman with a sense of destiny which would help her discover and fulfill her God given purpose.

Now, the third book of the WOW! Women trilogy emerged as WOW! Women of Legacy. Following tradition, I gave the blueprint for Women of Legacy in the last chapter, Leaving a Legacy.

In this book, WOW! Women of Legacy we use legacy terminology. The individual lessons are introduced or reinforced to, simply build the faith of God's woman in realizing her value, fulfilling her destiny and building a legacy to leave.

In each *Beginning A Legacy* and *Building Your Legacy* section throughout the book, I aspire to draw a map respectively using a woman's pattern of power, royal call to rule, war with words, will to win, torch of life and a life well lived, all as instructional building blocks in living a life of legacy.

None of us want to miss the mark or fumble in passing the torch. We want to walk out our God-appointed course and finish it in victory. Therefore, the Strengthening Your Legacy portion was written to concisely emphasize points to strengthen our legacy, as we go.

Realizing the world is not a perfect place but one of struggle and conflict of opposing forces, I have chosen to present contrasting aspects of the seven steps to legacy in each A Legacy of… and Legacy Snippet segments.

I seek to see women know there will be challenges in their lives yet at the same time remain confident that with God on their side they are well able to overcome every challenging circumstance (Can't you hear the voice of wisdom? She is standing at the city gates and at every crossroad, and at the door of every house. Listen to what she says.)

Recognizing faith without works is dead, the Summing It All Up portions are designed to sum it all up and help you apply God's Word in your life. We have learned in applying God's word to our lives, taking an action step is most important. So, a new section called Legacy Challenge has been added to encourage you take action.

Finally, you must know it's now a tradition, my faith always makes an appointment with Father God for our time together. I believe He will again meet us in each chapter and by His Spirit shatter images that say no to your prosperity, purpose, power and legacy in God. He has already said YES and AMEN to every promise.

So, let's journey together through WOW! Women of LEGACY to fulfill every plan, purpose, destiny and then pass it to the next generation. He has reserved a happy ending for our lives. (Jeremiah 29:11) So, come on; let's walk together through WOW! Women of Legacy.

Earma Brown

Chapter One

Leaving A Legacy

A Woman's Pattern Of Power

And the king loved Esther and she found favor beyond all the other women,
so he put on her the queen's crown. —*Esther 2:17*

sther was a distinctive young woman. One of the translations of Esther
means 'star.' Esther emerged as a star of her generation and left a legacy
of leadership, godliness, selflessness and walking in her newly received
royalty with grace and compassion. She faced the circumstances of her birth
as an orphan and position with courage and hope. She was an obedient and
highly favored young woman prepared for her Kairos moment, a night of
destiny with the king.

In part Esther's story began, When the time was fulfilled for Esther
daughter of Aminadab, the brother of Mordecai's father, to go in to the king,
she neglected none of the things that Gai, the eunuch in charge of the
women, had commanded. Now Esther found favor in the eyes of all who
saw her.

So Esther went in to King Artaxerxes in the twelfth month, which is
Adar, in the seventh year of his reign. And the king loved Esther and she
found favor beyond all the other virgins, so he put on her the queen's diadem.
Join me as we uncover the biblical principles of developing the seeds of
destiny given to each of us.

Beginning A Legacy

YOU Are A Shining Star!

Those who are wise will shine like the brightness of the heavens, and those who lead many to righteousness, like the stars for ever and ever. —Daniel 12:3

Esther, an orphan rose to the full potential of her name, in some languages translated as 'star.' Her fame propelled her to the highest position of any woman in her day. Even through biblical history, her legacy and example reaches through the generations. Like Esther, regardless of our status in life, we are called to be a shining star, leaving a legacy of a life well lived.

Years ago, for a season the Holy Spirit would pull a certain set of words up in my spirit. I would wake up with the jingle in my mind and heart, "You are a shining star..." but couldn't remember the words. Fortunately, my husband Varn, a musician from childhood has a talent for remembering almost all the songs he hears and have heard. That in itself is amazing to me. This song was no different.

You're a shining star, no matter who you are— Shining bright to see what you can truly be—You're a shining star no matter who you are— Shining bright to see what you can truly be... Let me tell a cautionary tale, so to speak. I'm not endorsing this group. For they were a secular music group. Since, the Holy Spirit used it to prompt me in this teaching, I'm giving you a little background and history, even though you probably don't need it. (smile)

"Shining Star" is a 1975 song by Earth, Wind & Fire from their album That's the Way of the World. The song was written by Maurice White, Larry Dunn and Philip Bailey and produced by White. "Shining Star" was Earth, Wind & Fire's first major hit, hitting No. 1 on both the U.S. Hot 100 and R&B charts.2

In 1975, Earth, Wind & Fire The Shining Star song hit the charts at U.S. Billboard Hot 100 at #1. Shining Star" won Earth, Wind & Fire a Grammy for Best R&B Performance by a Duo or Group with Vocals.

The little snippet of the song served as a thread that I followed to the word of God to see what he says about us being stars. It became a prophetic riddle in my life. I hope it does for you too. Here are a couple scriptures that say we are called to be shining stars in God's kingdom:

1.   Those who are wise will shine like the brightness of the heavens, and those who lead many to righteousness, like the stars for ever and ever.3

2.   And the teachers and those who are wise shall shine like the brightness of the firmament, and those who turn many to righteousness (to uprightness and right standing with God) [shall give forth light] like the stars forever and ever.4

3.   So that no one can criticize you. Live clean, innocent lives as children of God, shining like bright stars in a world full of crooked and perverse people.5

4.   "You are the light of the world. A town built on a hill cannot be hidden.6

Star Power: Memorize Meditate Speak

Now that we know we are called to be stars for Jesus, here are six confessions to memorize, meditate, and speak over yourself and others in your life.

1. I am a shining star for Jesus. May any fame I attain reflect Christ to a dark world. "So that no one can criticize you. Live clean, innocent lives as children of God, shining like bright stars in a world full of crooked and perverse people."7

2. I radiate light wherever I go. "You are the light of the world. A town built on a hill cannot be hidden."8

3. I shine like a firework in the night. "Then you will shine among them like stars in the sky." 9

4. I am a daughter of Light. "You are all children of the light and children of the day. We do not belong to the night or to the darkness."10

5. I am the salt of the earth. "You are the salt of the earth."11

6. I am a vessel of His Light. "For God, who said, "Let light shine out of darkness," made his light shine in our hearts to give us the light of the knowledge of God's glory displayed in the face of Christ."12

7. Beams and light and joy exude from within me. "Light shines on the godly, and joy on those whose hearts are right."13

After you embrace your self-worth, your beauty and joy in Christ, you have the fearlessness and fierceness to step into your destiny and reign... For more affirmations and declarations, visit http://wowontheweb.com for the WOW! Women Manifesto and how to create your own manifesto inside printable WOW! Women of Legacy Small Group Study Guide.

Building Your Legacy

God's Story Of Recompense

For the LORD has a day of vengeance, a year of recompense for Zion's cause.
— Isaiah 34:8

Esther's story in part, continues with Father God's intervention as Jehovah Gmolah, the Lord of Recompense. Through Esther's faith and perseverance, along with Mordecai and the nation of Israel God told the story of recompense.

The prevailing story resounds through the generations. Father God proclaims, "Vengeance is mine, I always recompense. The Roman writer confirms his words, "Beloved, never avenge yourselves, but leave it to the wrath of God, for it is written, 'Vengeance is mine, I will repay, says the Lord.'"

On that note, have you noticed Father God takes up for His people? He wants you to know, He not only has your back; He has a payback designed just for you. I've learned God doesn't waste any of our pain or troubles. He's a God that compensates and even repays you for your works, good or bad. Prophet Jeremiah declares, "For the Lord is the God of recompense. He will surely repay."

I've discovered recompense is one of the laws of the kingdom of God. Remember, the sowing and reaping law. I think we (the Body of Christ) and the world are familiar with this one by now. You know what goes around, comes around. What you sow, you shall reap. So, it is with His vengeance and His recompense. Hey, you didn't say anything about vengeance.

Yeah, I know but they go hand in hand. Father God said, "Vengeance is Mine. And I always recompense. So, it's important for you to know or remember that you don't have to hate. You don't have to get even. Like I said, God's got your back. Just keep on forgiving when someone wrongs you. But watch what God does. It's God's way to trouble those that trouble you... But I'm getting a little ahead of myself. I don't want to miss the foundation I'm about to lay so let me back up.

Going back to the story of Cain and Abel, we see the law of recompense in effect. It was the law of recompense that demanded justice for Abel's right sacrifice and his wrongful death. Many of you know how this story ends. Just in case you are new to the stories of the Bible, Abel offered right sacrifice and Cain offered sacrifice that was not pleasing to God.

Cain murdered his brother Abel. God judged Cain for his sin and wrong actions. Apart from Adam and Eve, it's one of the first pictures of recompense and retribution. Even so, I encourage you to read the story of Cain and Abel with fresh eyes and with the law of recompense in mind.16

Years ago, as a new Christian I went through a season of extremely troubling circumstances. I was severely persecuted on my job by my boss. One day, after a meeting with other managers, the others were filing out laughing and talking.

He walked up to me and whispered, "You should pack your bags now. Start looking for another job because I'm going to make sure you quit." I was shocked. That afternoon, I was in an accident. A drunk driver ran into the rear end of my car.

It sent me and my vehicle into a tail spin, like a spinning top. All I could do was hold on to the steering wheel. My car stopped within inches of the big picture window of a nearby restaurant. The people ran out and delivered me from the drunk driver. He had climbed out of his car, fussing and wagging his finger at me for driving in front of him on a red light.

The truth was, I had no idea. My mind was still reeling from the words my manager had just whispered to me.

He made my job and life miserable. But with God's help, I never quit. When I came through this season, I was grateful. But because of lack of wisdom and understanding about God, I felt hurt, abandoned and disappointed that He had not intervened and taken me out of this unwarranted trouble.

Instead, I was allowed to go through and suffered great loss. (Sound familiar?) I kept going over the scenes and episodes in my mind. Until finally one day in a vision He showed me the exact repayment of troubles my enemies had received. And a glimpse of me in a new workplace, laughing and enjoying life. I woke up with the words in my spirit from God, "I always recompense!"

For me, that day my journey began with learning about God's recompense, even His law of recompense. I had never heard the word recompense used to apply to anything in my natural world. No one had said to me, "I recompense you." To help expand our understanding of God's recompense, Webster defines it to mean: to repay or reward; to compensate as in a loss, etc.

Not long ago, Father God said to me, "The Days of Recompense have come." Knowing God gifts us with many different seasons, I immediately began to think about what He taught me over the years about His recompense. My heart was stirred in faith and expectancy about this season of God's recompense.

I want to share a little of it now. So, you can begin to look around with the same hope and expectancy of what God is doing in our life as Christian women. Perhaps you'll find that he has been speaking to you already about the same thing.

If not, I have good news! If you've been going through troubles and especially unwarranted trouble, you can expect God's recompense. You have a payback, even a compensation coming. Here's five things I've learned about God's law of recompense:

1. The law of recompense. I call it a law because He said, "I always recompense." In Scripture, just like his other laws it's applied to the just and unjust. Remember, God is a good god. He rains on the just and the unjust. His sun shines on the obedient and the disobedient.

Recompense and retribution are applied to every man, the just and the unjust. It is up to us (humanity), whether we receive reward, benefits and protection or penalties, punishments and judgments.17

2. Two sides to recompense. Even though recompense is applied to every man, there are two sides of recompense and retribution. One side is reward and the other is punishment. Rev. Brown wrote it so eloquently, "As long as we are in obedience to His Word, we receive the benefits and protection (rewards) of God's law of recompense.

But when we are living in disobedience, we inadvertently open ourselves to the judgments and even punishments of the law." (Proverbs 12:13,1)

3. The battle is the Lord's. I've learned if you want to receive God's recompense, you can't get out there and fight for yourself. If you've been wrongfully troubled, accused, mistreated you must forgive and allow Father God to fight the battle. Don't hold a hateful grudge; walk in forgiveness and know revenge belongs to God.

The writer of Romans said it like this, "Avenge not yourselves, beloved, but give place unto the wrath of God; for it is written, Vengeance belongeth unto me; I will recompense, saith the Lord." (Rom. 12:19)

4. Will God remember to recompense? Many have asked, myself included, "Why so long to recompense?" First of all, God is sovereign. Meaning His timing is perfect. I'm glad He's God and I'm not. In general, I'm glad man is not in charge of such things.

The Apostle Peter said it well, "The Lord is not slack concerning His promise, as some count slackness, but is longsuffering toward us, not willing that any should perish but that all should come to repentance." (2 Peter 3:9) The writer of Hebrews puts it another way, "For God is not unjust to forget your work and labor of love which you have shown toward His name, in that you have ministered to the saints and do minister." (Hebrews 6:10)

5. Recompense by Faith. There is no room for boasting. None of us can say, hey I've done everything right so recompense me God. Remember, all of us only entered in right relationship with God through Christ. The shed blood of Christ ultimately satisfied the requirements of God's justice (law of recompense).

In other words, you can shout right here! When you accepted Christ into your heart, you made a covenant with God. You are in right relationship with Him and eligible for His promises of recompense. His recompense includes working all things to your good; it means He will not waste a drop of your pain and troubles.

Just as He did Job, he will pay you back double. Just like Mordecai, He will be careful to honor and exalt you in due season. Because you share in Christ suffering, the law of recompense says you share in His glory.

And just like he proclaimed to me, when we've been treated unjustly, he always recompenses. It has not escaped his attention. Since, our thoughts and ways are not like God's we don't always understand.

But you can be sure he has purpose in just intentions for your life. His plans are for your good. He plans an expected end, even a bright future ahead for you. So, don't lose hope. Look to the hills from whence your help comes from.

As the Holy Spirit begins to point to examples of recompense around you, my hope is that your faith begins to grow to receive all that God has reserved for you. You can look for it; expect it and receive God's recompense by faith.

Strengthening Your Legacy

Living Life As A Pattern To Follow

For He foreordained us (destined us), planned in love for us to be adopted (revealed) as His own children through Jesus Christ, in accordance with the purpose of His will—because it pleased Him and was His kind intent. — Ephesians 1:5b

Esther's actions left a pattern of courage and loyalty to her people that we can take example from in our day. The Bible book Esther named after her is one of the few books dedicated to a story with a woman as the main character. Many researchers and scholars have said, it was not intended to be there.

According to them, it was deemed a novella, therefore, it was only by accident that it appears in the modern day translated Bibles. That may or may not be so, I'm just thankful it made it. I suspect it was Father God's plan all along. He loves confounding the wise with so called foolishness. Besides, it's a wonderful story of His recompense.

Have you created something using a pattern? You know; did you use a template or a blueprint to make it easier. Most everyone enjoys using a template to jumpstart their creations. My mother used patterns to sew clothing and quilts when my sisters, brothers and I were children. I remember sitting by her side and watching her unfold the patterns, laying them out on the table or floor. Then she would carefully study and cut each piece of cloth to make sure it was measured exactly to the specs of the pattern. It was a joy to see her finished products of dresses, suits and beautiful quilts.

Perhaps, its why I use patterns even now in my life in various ways. I use patterns, systems, templates, recipes, formulas to make my life easier. I love them. It often gives me the jumpstart I need to get things done quickly in excellence. I realized a long time ago, I can't be a master at everything. Therefore, to shorten my learning curve when I don't have the time to master a task or don't want to master it. I look for an easy template to jumpstart my work.

Not long ago, I discovered God uses patterns in our lives. Remember, all of humanity was started with the creation of one man and woman. Yes, we are created uniquely and wonderfully but in a similar pattern to Adam and Eve.

And now just as importantly, he expects us to become more and more a pattern to other believers. The Apostle Paul in a letter to the Philippians' believers encouraged them to pattern their lives after him and take note of others that lived up to his example. Then again, he encourages Pastor Timothy and now us with his words, "Hold tightly to the pattern of truth I taught you, especially concerning the faith and love of Jesus Christ offers you.

Guard well the splendid, God given ability you received as a gift from the Holy Spirit who lives within you."

Through the Apostle Paul and other Scripture writers, God commands us to pattern our lives after those who have ran their race well and now have gone on before us. Lately, I've been examining what kind of legacy I'm leaving or even what kind of example am I living in the now? I want to make sure I'm laying a good and worthy pattern for the believers in my circle.

How about you, dear friend? Are you a good example for your family and those in your circle of influence? Won't you join me in laying a good pattern of diligence, of being a good soldier enduring hardships of the season, making ourselves content in whatever circumstance we face or enjoy.

Link arms with me in showing ourselves as a hard worker, training for excellence in communicating the gospel and as a patient farmer in the Kingdom of God sowing and reaping in due season. —Philippians 3:17

A Legacy of Love

Returning To Our First Love

In the Gospels the Apostle Paul likened our life to a race," Therefore we also, since we are surrounded by so great a cloud of witnesses, let us lay aside every weight, and the sin which so easily ensnares us, and let us run with endurance the race that is set before us." —Hebrews 12:1, NKJV

Have you realized when you drift away from God, you always stay longer than you anticipated and you go further than you ever thought you would go?

That's exactly what happened to me as a teenager. I loved to read Bible stories as a five-year-old. There was a prayer of salvation at the back of the book.

I prayed it and received Christ at an early age. Then as a teen-ager, I walked away from God and said I'll be back. In Christianese, you could say I back-slid.

I won't go into it but I can tell you my life took a downward spiral after that. You veteran Christians know the result of that decision. Anyway, on with my story.

First Love

Twenty-four years later, in 1987 I was a discount retail manager in the New Orleans and Louisiana area. I got promoted and my company moved me to the Gulf Coast of Mississippi. I was so excited that I would be living a few miles from the ocean. Little did I know something bigger than that was brewing; my life was about to change forever.

One of my fellow managers in the area started to talk to me about God. I had already spouted out that he could talk to me about God but no preaching. I told him I hadn't listened to any preaching in over fifteen years and I wasn't about to start now.

He kept talking anyway. Sometimes, I would get up and leave. One day through a word of knowledge he said, "Father God said he wants you back. You said you would be back. He says he wants you back. Then he began to tell me a story. It was a story I read over and over again as a child. I read it scores of times.

He went on to say, "He says you'll recognize this story." He started to tell me the story of Saul of Tarsus who became Paul the Apostle. He reminded me of how Saul was busy breathing out threats and persecution of the Christians. And how a light shone from heaven blinded him and knocked him from his horse…Of course, after reading it nearly a hundred times I remembered immediately. I jumped up and said, "You're scaring me now. No one could know those things about me."

Later that night, I began to think about what happened. I began to wonder how it would be being back with the Lord. Could it even happen? Hadn't I gone too far to ever be retrieved, to ever change? The rest is history. Weeks later, when I saw my friend again I was ready. He led me in a prayer. I recommitted my life to God. I accepted Christ as my Lord and Savior.

When Did You Commit To Christ

Which brings me to the question I have for you. Do you remember when you committed to Christ? Were you a youngster, a middle aged adult or did you make a serious commitment, recently? Either way, you might consider marking that day; you know write it down, even memorialize it. Why? Because you may need to refer to it along the way. When it gets tough or you get weary, it can be inspiration—food for your journey.

At last, you need to pass it to the next generation. When they ask why is that day so special to you—you can tell them about your decision for Christ and what it means to you.

Remember the Israelites, Father God periodically would have them create a memorial for something. For example, when they first crossed the Jordan River into the Promised Land he commanded them to have twelve priests each select a stone from the river bed and create a memorial on the bank.

They created a twelve stone memorial so that when their children would ask about it, they could tell the story of how God as a shepherd brought his people from Egypt into the Promised Land.

I'm serious; if you can't mark a day, a year or even a season when you first believed or your heart was changed for Christ, you might need to return to your first love. Do an X marks the spot—I first committed my life to Christ.

Go over your story once again. Write down or record your testimony, at least tell it to someone afresh. Give them the short version. Don't overload them with every detail but do give it.

First Volunteered In Local Church

There's another decision I want to talk to you about, for the same reason. Here's the question. Do you remember when you first decided to serve God in your local church? When was the first time you volunteered in church or served on the Usher, Hospitality team or Children's ministry?

Remember the first things. Think about how excited you were to do the things of God. Consider why you do what you do? Did you realize it was God prompting you, leading you to do what you do?

I remember back in Mississippi, my pastor asked me to help count the offerings on Sunday and serve on an accounting team that met once a week to take care of church business. I was new in the church and didn't agree at first.

To be honest, I had some wrong ideas about serving in church. I already worked long hours on my job. So in my mind why should I do that with no expectation of pay? But willing to change, I asked God what he thought about it.

It Is God At Work In You

Our friend and advocate the Holy Spirit spoke these simple words of Scripture to me, "...for it is God who is at work in you, both to will and to work for His good pleasure." –Philippians 2:13b

On through the years, it has been the source of my zeal—my relationship with Christ and His command through the Holy Spirit and Scripture that it is Him working through us all (as we allow Him) to do His will and good pleasure.

I've served in many different capacities by His leading and eventually became a servant leader that our books and ministry were birthed from. You can read more of our servant leadership story in our latest book 'In The Spirit of Leadership by Varn Brown.

In closing, I encourage you to return to your first love and mark it. Even create a memorial, a testimony to encourage you when you're weary in the battle. And above all to pass it to the next generation. Stir up the zeal of God to do His will! The Hebrew writer said it best, "who saved us and called us to a holy calling not because of our works but because of his own purpose and grace which he gave us in Christ Jesus before the ages began." —2 Timothy 1:9

Legacy Snippet

7 Ways To Live Your Legacy

Let each generation tell its children of your mighty acts; let them proclaim your power. —Psalm 145:4

Are you designing your life as a torch? With your eye on the next generation, you've decided, no matter what, you want to live your life well as an example. There's good news! You can live a life of legacy. God is a god of the generations. He is the same yesterday, today and forever. Through God's plan, this generation prepares and passes the torch to the next. Inside this book series, you will discover seven steps to prepare and live your life as a legacy:

1. Leaving A Legacy for Generations To Come: A Woman's Pattern Of Power. We begin our new study with Esther, a shining star of her generation. Her fame and legacy still make a great pattern for us to follow.

2. Tapping Into Your Inner Queen: A Woman's Royal Call To Rule. Queen of Sheba and her entourage arrived in Israel to visit King Solomon to further her education and receive what was valued above silver and gold. She came bearing elephantine piles of gifts to honor and gain access to wisdom, knowledge and insight beyond what she could ask or imagine…

3. Breaking The Generational Curse: A Woman's War Using Words. Learn the power of life and death in your words. Discover how to break the curse running rampant through the generations of your family.

4. Overcoming the Giants of Your Generation: A Woman's Will To Win. Re-discover the power of choice and a will to win. We examine the choices Ruth and Orpah and legacy they respectively left. Find out how to overcome the giants of your generations, once and for all.

5. Passing the Torch of Legacy: A Woman's Torch Of Legacy. Use Lois and Eunice as an example. Study how to prepare your life as a torch to be passed by living your life in his will and way.

6. Living the Legacy: A Woman's Life Well Lived. Discover how to live your life as a legacy to pass to the next generation.

7. THRIVE: A discipleship and mentorship program for WOW! Women all over the world. See how to join, make your mark and pass it on. Visit WOW! Women Global for details http://wowwomenglobal.com

"Father God desires the same for each generation. God said to Moses, "I AM WHO I AM"; and He said, "Thus you shall say to the sons of Israel, 'I AM has sent me to you.'" God, furthermore, said to Moses, "Thus you shall say to the sons of Israel, 'The LORD, the God of your fathers, the God of Abraham, the God of Isaac, and the God of Jacob, has sent me to you.' This is My name forever, and this is My memorial-name to all generations. Exodus 3:14,15

Father God has put in each of us a blueprint, the thoughts, plans and desire for a bright future," explains Earma. "I have designed the WOW! Women message to hopefully position the reader to receive God's plans to satisfy that longing," Start your journey today using the seven lessons in everything you do and experience the joy of creating a life full of passion, purpose and power in God then leaving a legacy of a life well-lived.

Summing It All Up

Have realized you are a shining star? A little girl was born in a time of turmoil for Israel. She was an orphan with no future and no destiny. Or so it seemed, what happened next could have changed her future and the generations to come. But Esther learned a secret that brought salvation to her nation with an unexpected upset of her enemies' plans, so powerful that it echoes through the centuries.

Esther embraced her preparation season and followed the instructions from her mentors to the letter. It worked and she was ready for her Kairos season. She even discovered the real reason for her journey, to save a people. She used every ounce of her skill, discernment, wisdom, knowledge and all that had prepared her for such a time as this.

She stepped out in faith, prayed, fasted and received miraculous strategy to war against the evil intent of Israel's foes. Yet none of it would have done any good, if she hadn't taken the courage to act. Now it's your turn. Get started building your legacy by living it right now.

Through the generations, we take example from a woman who rose to stardom, even royalty from the meager beginnings of an orphan.

Legacy Challenge 1:

Log in at http://wowotheweb.com and pick up your copy of the WOW! Women of Legacy's crown logo and put it on your website and blog. Continue in your QUEEN training and reign as you go.

Chapter Two

Tap Into Your Inner Queen

A Woman's Royal Call To Rule

For we are God's handiwork, created in Christ Jesus to do good works, which God prepared in advance for us to do." —Ephesians 2:10

An Ethiopian Queen and her entourage filed before the throne of King Solomon. They came in respect, bearing an elephantine load of gifts. They were expecting a return on their investment. What they received surprised a nation and is still heralded today as spectacular.

This Ethiopian queen acted as an example for women today. She pursued and received something that many don't value. She left with more gifts than she had brought and one in particular stood above the rest. She left with an education.

Queen Sheba is famous for her pursuit of knowledge and wisdom. In fact, on hear-say she travelled from across the world to experience the wisdom and understanding of King Solomon.

Like Queen Sheba with King Solomon, the wisest man on earth, we thirst for an understanding, wisdom, knowledge and a better way in life. Through Christ and the Parakletos, the Holy Spirit He sent us, we get to draw from Father God, the Rock of Ages-great grandfather of King David.

☙

Beginning A Legacy

10 Ways To Tap Into Your Inner Queen

And we who have received the gift of righteousness do reign as a queen in life by Jesus Christ —Romans 5:17 para.

Now when the Queen of Sheba heard of the fame of Solomon concerning the name of the LORD, she came to test him with hard questions. She came to Jerusalem with a very great retinue, with camels bearing spices, and very much gold, and precious stones; and when she came to Solomon, she told him all that was on her mind.

And Solomon answered all her questions; there was nothing hidden from the king which he could not explain to her. And when the queen of Sheba had seen all the wisdom of Solomon, the house that he had built, the food of his table, the seating of his officials, and the attendance of his servants, their clothing, his cupbearers, and his burnt offerings which he offered at the house of the LORD, there was no more spirit in her.

And she said to the king, "The report was true which I heard in my own land of your affairs and of your wisdom, but I did not believe the reports until I came and my own eyes had seen it; and, behold, the half was not told me; your wisdom and prosperity surpass the report which I heard. Happy are your wives! Happy are these your servants, who continually stand before you and hear your wisdom! Blessed be the LORD your God, who has delighted in you and set you on the throne of Israel! Because the LORD loved Israel forever, he has made you king, that you may execute justice and righteousness."

Then she gave the king a hundred and twenty talents of gold, and a very great quantity of spices, and precious stones; never again came such an abundance of spices as these which the Queen of Sheba gave to King Solomon. Moreover, the fleet of Hiram, which brought gold from Ophir, brought from Ophir a very great amount of almug wood and precious stones.

And the king made of the almug wood supports for the house of the LORD, and for the king's house, lyres also and harps for the singers; no such almug wood has come or been seen, to this day.

And King Solomon gave to the Queen of Sheba all that she desired, whatever she asked besides what was given her by the bounty of King Solomon. So she turned and went back to her own land, with her servants. -1 Kings 10:1-13 For now, here are those ten ways to tap into your inner queen:

1. Reverence God. Start with right priorities. Put God first in your life. Reverence him for what he is to you, right now. For example, I start my prayer time with reverencing God for being Jehovah Jireh, the Lord God who provides for me and my family. Then I reverence him for being Jehovah Gmolah, the God of recompense. At WOW Women Global, we are starting a challenge of 21 Days of blessings and recompense. Here's one more, he is a sure foundation for every circumstance; he's a rich store of salvation, wisdom and knowledge. I reverence Father God and draw out all that I need.

2. Seek wisdom and knowledge from God. Do you have any problems in your life that need solutions? If you're anything like me, there's always challenges and things that need to be worked out. If you haven't before, ask the Holy Spirit for wisdom. Jesus sent him as our helper, you know. He is our parakletos. The Greek word translated "Comforter" or "Counselor" (as found in John 14:16, 26; 15:26; and 16:7) is parakletos. Try it today. Ask for God's wisdom about anything you've been trying to work out for days, months. For some, it's been years. I know you gave up. You have a better understanding now. Pray again.

3. Get an understanding. An understanding will protect the word of God in your heart. For me, an understanding comes when I meditate on the word of God or something the Holy Spirit has said to me. As I roll it over in my mind or think about the possibilities. Recently, in conversation it will pop up, an understanding of the matter. I'll start by asking, what do you think about this, my husband or a trusted friend.

4. Educate yourself. Don't be afraid of education. All education doesn't have to come from a college or university. Go get a degree, certification, license or training for a skill or even a trade. If God is prompting, you. You can do it.

5. Guard against the enemy's theft of your UNDERSTANDING. The word of God says, he the devil, is after it immediately. For he knows most times, with an understanding comes a change of heart, a change of attitude or a perspective flip. Remember in the parable of the seed and the sower, the enemy came quickly to try and steal the seed.

6. Rehearse your victories. Remind yourself of the times you were successful. There are bound to be times you felt on top. You know you were strong, fierce and confident. Think on those times. What were you doing? What victories and successes did you enjoy?

7. Stand firm in your faith. Remember, when you first believed. Reassess why you believe what you believe. It's a good time to write your confession of faith or your manifesto. If you've never written a manifesto, be sure to review the 'How To Write A Manifesto' in the WOW! Women of Destiny at http://wowontheweb.com

8. Stop comparing yourself with others. You are unique. Each of us are on our own journey. Father God is big enough and compassionate enough to know us individually. Yes, it's a mystery. You don't have to understand everything to believe it. We, women usually compare ourselves negatively to someone else. So, if you are there, stop it, now. I can say that with authority because I was there until I stopped.

9. Know where your strength comes from. The Bible is full of mysterious contradictions and oxymorons. In Christ, we can say it and mean it, "Let the weak say I am strong. Like the Apostle Paul, "Each time he said, "My grace is all you need. My power works best in weakness." So now I am glad to boast about my weaknesses, so that the power of Christ can work through me." -2 Corinthians 12:9

10. Reshape your image. Use the affirmations, confessions and the word of God to change your inner image. Before you know it, you become the victor and not the victim. Throughout the books, I have always given you good affirmations and confessions to use. They work but you have to use them. Consider creating a manifesto of your favorite affirmations.

Have you assumed your throne? Do you see yourself as queenly yet? You know, queens don't beg. For us, we walk in our God-given authority. Queens don't have bad self-esteem. We find and walk in our worth in Christ. We know we are accepted in the Beloved. Queens don't self-depreciate. We take hold of ourselves; we don't bash ourselves or each other.

Queens know they are royalty. Queens train in knowing their duties. Queens pursue knowledge and wisdom for themselves and their kingdom. In other words, a queen pursues a further education for herself and her people. We know we are created in the image and likeness of Father God. Therefore, we know that we are creative. We are smart, educated women, always looking for new and innovative ideas.

Building Your Legacy

A Woman's Real Beauty

Is your inner person beautiful in Christ? We all know what beautiful means in our natural world. Something or someone pleasing to the eyes is a good definition of physical beauty. Have you thought about what it means to be beautiful in spirit? Do you know if you are pleasing in God's eyes? (Beautiful)

You might remember from Scripture that faith is what pleases God. The Hebrew writer put it like this, "Without faith it is impossible to please Him..." (Hebrews 11:5) Although, God expects us to participate in good works and to even spur each other to good works.

He does not expect us to work for the things he has given us freely. He has given us salvation, the gifts of the spirit and all good things pertaining to life in abundance.

I prefaced with all that because I don't want you to feel you have to work harder to become beautiful in God's eyes. It's not a works thing. It's a faith thing. Remember, Father God called Jesus, His beloved Son before he ever did a thing in ministry.

You need only put on the garments of righteousness he has supplied us through Christ. A few of the garments of Christ are kindness, gentleness, longsuffering, love and faith. Here are seven tips on beautifying our spirit in Christ.

1.   **Grow in gentleness.** Whether we are man or woman, we can take a lesson from the Apostle Peter as he instructs women, "Do not let your adornment be merely outward-arranging the hair, wearing gold, or putting on fine apparel-rather let it be the hidden person of the heart (your spirit) with the incorruptible beauty of a gentle and quiet spirit, which is very precious in the sight of God."

2.   **Build a good testimony.** Serve in faith and your testimony will become more and more that you please God. Our faith in action pleases God. Whether it's good or bad, faithful or faithless, we are all working on our testimony before God. Again I refer to the Hebrew writer who said, "Now faith is the substance of things hoped for, the evidence of things not seen.

For by it the elders obtained a good testimony." And later he goes on to say, "By faith Enoch was taken away so that he did not see death...for before he was taken he had this testimony, that he pleased God."

3.   **Put on Christ.** The Roman writer says, "Clothe yourselves with the Lord Jesus." (Romans 13:14) You may ask, "How do I put on Christ." I'm so glad you asked. You put on Christ by renewing your mind. The more we read our Bible and pray, the more our mind becomes renewed to the Word of God.

We begin to think like our Lord; we begin to act like our God. In Ephesians, the Apostle Paul encourages the Ephesians church, now us with, "...that you put off, concerning your former conduct, the old man which grows corrupt, according to the deceitful lusts, and be renewed in the spirit of your mind, and that you put on the new man which was created according to God in true righteousness and holiness.

4.   **Wear the clothing of righteousness.** I mentioned earlier the Apostle Peter instructing us to focus more on our inner beauty than our outward appearance. We must daily put on our garments of kindness and patience. The Apostle Paul writing to the Colossian church encouraging them to put on the character of the new man (inner man), "Therefore, as the elect of God, holy and beloved, put on tender mercies, kindness, humility, meekness, longsuffering... (Colossians 3:12)

44

5.   **Be humble.** King David was known as a man after God's heart. He pleased God through humility. He was considered humble not because he never made a mistake. In fact, he's more famous for making some big blunders (sin) than being a humble man. King David is recorded as humble and pleasing to God because when he sinned, he repented and received forgiveness in faith. So while you're cultivating humility remember this, "For the Lord takes pleasure in His people; He will beautify the humble with salvation." (Psalm 149:4)

6.   **Grow in God's Favor.** You may be surprised as I was to discover another word that interchanges with favor is beauty. More and more, realize God has already given us His unmerited favor-His grace. We can do nothing more to deserve it. So just receive it by faith along with all the other free gifts like salvation, mercy and forgiveness that He has given us through Christ. The Psalmist says it well, "And let the beauty (favor) of the Lord our God be upon us, and establish the work of our hands for us; yes, establish the work of our hands. (Psalm 90:17)

7.   **Look at the Lord as Beautiful.** The man after God's heart puts it like this, "One thing I have desired of the Lord, that will I seek; that I may dwell in the house of the Lord all the days of my life, to behold the beauty of the Lord." Psalm 27:4 When we begin to recognize none of us can be beautiful or righteousness except through Christ, we begin to see the beauty of our Lord. We will realize more and more that He is the only One that can give us beauty for the ashes of our lives. (Isaiah 61:3)

Begin to beautify yourself in Christ. You'll discover the more you grow in gentleness, build a good testimony, put on Christ, wear godly garments, become humble, and grow in God's favor, the more BEAUTIFUL you become.

Strengthening Your Legacy

15 Powerful Virtues of Understanding

Making your ear attentive to wisdom and inclining your heart to understanding; yes, if you call out for insight and raise your voice for understanding, if you seek it like silver and search for it as for hidden treasures, then you will understand the reverence of the Lord and find the knowledge of God. -Proverbs 2:2-5

Has God said to you lately, you're on your way to your destiny? You're going to the next level? If you're anything like me, you get all excited (as we should be) that you're going to the next level. You say praise God! I'm going to the next level. In case you haven't realized it yet, the next level is maturity.

I am considered a late bloomer with most things in my life. So, true to form when I turned forty, I began to seek God about understanding my purpose. I'm pretty sure most of my late blooming has to do with the detours I took earlier in life. Yet, Father God has been faithful to me.

So, I began to ask myself and then Father God, "Why am I here?" What is my purpose? In the process, I learned one of the biggest fears of people, in general, is to die having lived a meaningless life.

I must admit it didn't come to me immediately. I kept pursuing God in prayer. He began to speak to me about his general purpose for his creation 'woman.' You know the things he's given all of us inherently as men and women.

One common gift shared by all women stood above the others, is her gift of influence. It's the reason, my song became doing extraordinary with ordinary tools. I know you're wondering what all this has to do with the virtues of understanding. Stay with me, I'm going somewhere. You want to be around when we get there.

Eventually, like the dawning of a new day, understanding of my God given purpose came to me. Even more, I see the value of understanding. I encourage you to get understanding that leads to wisdom and maturity, in all you do. So, it's true, we receive better, we change better and we stay changed if we understand.

It's why one of the strongest things the proverbial writer said was in all your getting, get an understanding. The infamous story of Daniel, his tribulation and his 21-day fast was because he was seeking God for understanding about what was going on in his life and his nation's future.

He said to me, "O Daniel, you are very precious to God, understand the words that I am about to tell you and stand upright, for I have now been sent to you." And when he had spoken this word to me, I stood up trembling. 12Then he said to me, "Do not be afraid, Daniel, for from the first day that you set your heart on understanding this and on humbling yourself before your God, your words were heard, and I have come in response to your words....—Daniel 10:11,12

The definition of understanding: the ability to understand something; comprehension; sympathetically aware of other people's feelings; tolerant and forgiving. An informal agreement; an agreement of opinion or feeling; a friendly or harmonious relationship. A willingness to understand people's behavior and forgive them

Through research, success strategist all over the world say when we understand the Big Why to anything, including our life, we can succeed faster. It's why best-selling books, The Purpose Driven Life by Rick Warren and recently Finding Your Destiny by TD Jakes sell like hot cakes. And it's why one of my most popular WOW! Women books is Women of Destiny. If you're interested and don't have a copy, go to http://www.wowontheweb.com and get a copy. You can also purchase in bulk, if you choose lead a Bible study with it. Lots of women have been leading their women's ministry groups through it.

Anyway, there's power in getting a good understanding. It's God's way, knowledge and understanding leads to receiving wisdom. It's more important how we apply knowledge in understanding, than it is to get a bunch of knowledge. As you may know already, knowledge by itself has a tendency to puff up.

From Strong's Bible Dictionary #995, understand, bin (bean) To understand, discern, perceive, grasp, consider, regard, be perceptive, have insight. This verb occurs more than 165 times and refers to that intelligent process of perception, discernment and understanding., which all human beings possess in varying amounts.

From the word 'bin' is derived the noun *binah*, meaning understanding; this term occurs 37 times. Notice in Nehemiah the spiritual revival did not happen until the people clearly understood the word of God. They read from the Book of the Law of God and clearly explained the meaning of what was being read, helping the people understand each passage. - Nehemiah 8:8

With that said, to help us realize the value of understanding, here are fifteen of the twenty-one virtues of understanding.

1. Brings light. The unfolding of your words gives light; it imparts understanding to the simple. -Psalm 119:130

2. Reveals hidden treasure. Making your ear attentive to wisdom and inclining your heart to understanding; yes, if you call out for insight and raise your voice for understanding, if you seek it like silver and search for it as for hidden treasures, then you will understand the fear of the Lord and find the knowledge of God. -Proverbs 2:2-5

3. Leads to wisdom. In Col 1:9, Paul prays for the Church at Colosse, that they "might be filled with the knowledge of his will in all wisdom and spiritual understanding."

4. Builds your house (life). Proverbs 24:3,4, where we find that a house is builded by wisdom, established by understanding, and decorated by knowledge.

5. Promotes application of God's word. Faith without works (application of God's word) is dead--fruitless.

6. Gain long life. Blessed is the one who finds wisdom, and the one who gets understanding, for the gain from her is better than gain from silver and her profit better than gold. She is more precious than jewels, and nothing you desire can compare with her. Long life is in her right hand; in her left hand are riches and honor. Her ways are ways of pleasantness, and all her paths are peace... —Proverbs 3:13-18

7. Helps us choose the right way. Keep me from lying to myself; give me the privilege of receiving the knowledge of your instructions. I have chosen the way of faithfulness (God's Way - His Way); I set your rules before me.

8. Go to your destiny. I run in the path of your commands (Destiny), for you have broadened my understanding. Teach me your decrees, O LORD; I will keep them to the end.

9. Find your happy ending. Give me understanding and I will obey your instructions; I will put them into practice with all my heart. Make me walk along the path of your commands, for that is where my happiness is found.

10. Guard your happy life. Discretion will watch over you, understanding will guard you, delivering you from the way of evil, from men of perverted speech, who forsake the paths of uprightness to walk in the ways of darkness, who rejoice in doing evil and delight in the perverseness of evil, men whose paths are crooked, and who are devious in their ways... -Proverbs 2:11-16

11. Delight the Lord with understanding. Thus says the Lord: "Let not the wise man boast in his wisdom, let not the mighty man boast in his might, let not the rich man boast in his riches, but let him who boasts boast in this, that he understands and knows me, that I am the Lord who practices steadfast love, justice, and righteousness in the earth. For in these things I delight, declares the Lord."

12. Draw from the fountain of life with understanding. Good sense is a fountain of life to him who has it, but the instruction of fools is folly. —— Proverbs 16:22

13. Using godly fruit of self-control is a sign of a man of understanding. Proverbs 17:27 Whoever restrains his words has knowledge, and he who has a cool spirit is a man of understanding. —Proverbs 17:27

14. Thrive with knowledge, understanding and a gentle heart in God. They are darkened in their understanding, alienated from the life of God because of the ignorance that is in them, due to their hardness of heart. Ephesians 4:18

15. Develop a wellspring of life. Understanding is a wellspring of life to him who has it, but the correction of fools is folly. —Proverbs 16:22

16. Be open and look for new ideas. The intelligent woman is always open to new ideas. In fact, he looks for them. —Proverbs 18:15

17. Pray to be filled with the knowledge of God's will in all spiritual wisdom and understanding. And so, from the day we heard, we have not ceased to pray for you, asking that you may be filled with the knowledge of his will in all spiritual wisdom and understanding, so as to walk in a manner worthy of the Lord, fully pleasing to him, bearing fruit in every good work and increasing in the knowledge of God.

May you be strengthened with all power, according to his glorious might, for all endurance and patience with joy, giving thanks to the Father, who has qualified you to share in the inheritance of the saints in light. He has delivered us from the domain of darkness and transferred us to the kingdom of his beloved Son… -Colossians 1:9-29

So, getting knowledge and understanding alone should not be the main goal of our life. But, applying God's Word to our life is most important. James even says that faith without works (application) is a dead (unproductive) faith! (James 2:17)

I must add one word of caution, before I close this section, the virtues of understanding, in the kingdom of God many things are a mystery and we accept them by faith. It may or may not be connected with getting an understanding. Which is why even with receiving knowledge and understanding, we depend on the Holy Spirit to teach and guide us into how to apply all things concerning life in Christ. I charge you to continue growing in God through knowledge, understanding and wisdom, learning to apply his word to your life more and more. Now, go to your destiny in God and live your life as a legacy.

A Legacy of Wisdom

16 More Virtues of Wisdom Knowledge and Understanding

I keep asking that the God of our Lord Jesus Christ, the glorious Father, may give you the Spirit of wisdom and revelation, so that you may know him better. -Ephesians 1:17

Queen Sheba, a seeker, came away from Solomon's court filled with knowledge. In fact, while observing the inner workings of King Solomon's court, staff and his judgements, the story says she was overwhelmed.

Her pursuit of this education showed such great integrity and honesty that it is still heralded as spectacular today. The writer of Proverbs said it like this, "The mind of a person who has understanding is always ready to learn. Their ears and eyes are open and looking for knowledge." -Proverbs 18:15

In Colossians 1:9, the writer describes the Apostle Paul praying for the Church at Colosse, that they "might be filled with the knowledge of his will in all wisdom and spiritual understanding." And again in Ephesians 1:17, he prayed for the Saints, "I keep asking that the God of our Lord Jesus Christ, the glorious Father, may give you the Spirit of wisdom and revelation, so that you may know him better."

To grow as a Christian, requires a working knowledge of God's Word. With the line by line, precept by precept growth pattern, a "little knowledge" leads us to a "full knowledge", which leads us to "understanding", and finally to "wisdom."

The basic Greek word for "knowledge" is "gnosis." Gnosis is described loosely as a vertical list of facts. In 1 Corinthians 8:1, we discover "gnosis" by itself has a tendency to "puff up" or make one proud.

So, when the word of God commands us to grow in "knowledge," the Greek word is "epignosis" or a "full knowledge."

When we do it God's way, and grow in the knowledge of his Word bit by bit, it leads us to an "understanding", which is the Greek word "sunesis," which literally means "a flowing together of two rivers." Therefore, "Sunesis" becomes a picture of two of our lists of facts merging together and our understanding becoming deeper and wider.

In 2 Timothy 2:7, Paul says "consider what I say and the Lord give thee understanding (sunesis)." Knowledge and understanding leads us to "wisdom". The English word "wisdom" is a translation of the Greek word "Sophia," meaning the application of knowledge and understanding. God's Word does not tell us specifically to pray for knowledge, understanding, or even faith, but in James 1:5 we find "If any of you lack wisdom, let him ask of God, that giveth to all [men] liberally, and upbraideth not (doesn't fuss at us or find fault); and it shall be given him".

With that said, to help us realize the value of understanding, here are ten more virtues of understanding to learn from:

1. **Be strengthened with power** through his Spirit in your inner being

Ephesians 3:16-19 That according to the riches of his glory he may grant you to be strengthened with power through his Spirit in your inner being, so that Christ may dwell in your hearts through faith—that you, being rooted and grounded in love, may have strength to comprehend with all the saints what is the breadth and length and height and depth, and to know the love of Christ that surpasses knowledge, that you may be filled with all the fullness of God.

2. **Distinguish the things given to us freely by God.** Now we have received not the spirit of the world, but the Spirit who is from God, that we might understand the things freely given us by God. 1 Corinthians 2:1

3. **Know who the author of confusion masquerades as.** And no wonder, for even Satan disguises himself as an angel of light. -2 Corinthians 11:14

4. **Seek after God.** The Lord looks down from heaven on the children of man, to see if there are any who understand, who seek after God. They have all turned aside; together they have become corrupt; there is none who does good, not even one. —Psalm 14: 2-3

5. **Hear the voice of wisdom.** Does not wisdom call? Does not understanding raise her voice? -Proverbs 8:1

6. **Put away childish ways.** When I was a child, I spoke like a child, I thought like a child, I reasoned like a child. When I became a man, I gave up childish ways. For now, we see in a mirror dimly, but then face to face. Now I know in part; then I shall know fully, even as I have been fully known. So now faith, hope, and love abide, these three; but the greatest of these is love. 1 Corinthians 13:11–13

7. **Safeguard the seed of the word.** As for what was sown on good soil, this is the one who hears the word and understands it. He indeed bears fruit and yields, in one case a hundredfold, in another sixty, and in another thirty." —Matthew 13:23

8. **Give light (understanding) to the whole house.** Nor do people light a lamp and put it under a basket, but on a stand, and it gives light to all in the house. —Matthew 5:15

9. **Recognize Him That Is True.** And we know that the Son of God has come and has given us an understanding, that we may know Him who is true, and we are in Him who is true, in His Son Jesus Christ. This is the true God and eternal life. —1 John 5:20 NLT

10. **Allow Father God to open your mind.** Then he opened their minds so they could understand the Scriptures. —Luke 24:45

11. **Do all things through Christ.** I can do all things I need to do, everything that God calls me to do, through His Son Jesus Christ. —Phil 4:13

12. **Refuse to meditate too much on yourself.** Beware of having yourself on your mind too much. Don't meditate excessively on what you have done right or what you have done wrong. Both of these activities keep your mind on you!

Keep your thoughts centered on Christ and His principles: You will guard him and keep him in perfect and constant peace whose mind (both its inclination and its character) is stayed on You... —Isaiah 26:3.

13. Take care of yourself. Take good care of yourself physically. Take time to rest. It's good wisdom to rest. Do the best you can with what God gave you to work with—but don't be excessive or vain about your appearance.

14. Educate yourself but don't be prideful. Learn all you can, but don't allow your education to become a point of pride. God does not use us because of our education, but because of our heart toward him.

15. Acknowledge your gifts and talents are a gift from God. Realize that your gifts and talents are a gift, not something you have manufactured yourself. Don't look down on people who cannot do what you do.

16. Embrace your weaknesses. Don't despise your weaknesses—they keep us dependent upon God. In other words embrace your weakness through Christ.

In the Old Testament, we find the three words we've been discussing to build a life, in Proverbs 24:3,4, a house is built by wisdom, established by understanding, and decorated by knowledge.

The book of Proverbs is considered the book of application and the book James is the book of wisdom in the New Testament, and both are recommending us to apply God's Word to our lives. In the words of Apostle James, we are urged, even commanded to 'become doers of the word of God."

So, getting knowledge and understanding alone should not be the main goal of our life. But, applying God's Word to our life is most important. James even says that faith without works (application) is a dead (unproductive) faith! (James 2:17)

Legacy Snippet

Affirmations Fit For A Queen

Develop your Christ gift. Most of what God gives comes in seed form. I know there are exceptions, brilliant genius that are born with a ten talent gift. But most of us, have to work at it. We start out with normal proficiency. You doing what we can, when we can.

Then, if we keep developing, we come to an expert status. We don't let anything stop us. We keep going and going, until we arrive at genius level. For now, here are some affirmations fit for a Queen.

- **I am a victor.** "No, in all these things we are more than conquerors through him who loved us." —Romans 8:37

- **I have a heavenly calling.** "Therefore, holy brothers and sisters, who share in the heavenly calling, fix your thoughts on Jesus, whom we acknowledge as our apostle and high priest." —Hebrews 3:1

- **I have royalty in my veins and lead with integrity.** "But you are a chosen people, a royal priesthood, a holy nation, God's special possession, that you may declare the praises of him who called you out of darkness into his wonderful light." —1 Peter 2:9

- **I am designed for good works.** "For we are God's handiwork, created in Christ Jesus to do good works, which God prepared in advance for us to do." —Ephesians 2:10

- **I am a co-heir with Christ.** "Now if we are children, then we are heirs- heirs of God and co-heirs with Christ. If indeed we share in His sufferings in order that we may also share with His glory." —Romans 8:17

- **I am chosen and called by God to produce fruit.** "You did not choose me, but I chose you and appointed you so that you might go and bear fruit— fruit that will last—and so that whatever you ask in my name the Father will give you." —John 15:16

Now, speak the bolded declarations out loud to yourself. The power of life and death is in the tongue, so it is vital that you only allow the Truth to come out of your mouth. It could be the difference in an amazing life or a disappointing one. —Proverbs 18:21

Summing It All Up

Has your inner queen emerged? Whether she has or not, no worries. You may have discovered by now; our inner game takes time to develop. So, keep tapping into your inner queen until she shines forth, naturally, even fiercely.

I was inspired by Queen of Sheba's thirst for wisdom and knowledge. I was thrilled to discover queens are smart and they seek out new ideas and opportunities. No need to wait for your ship to come in. You can hire a shuttle boat, get in your row boat and sail out to the ship.

Either way, now is the time. Look what happened for Queen of Sheba and others like her, including me. Her thirst for knowledge led her to journey across the known world to an education fit for a queen. Eventually, it served as an example to women all over the world in many languages and worlds. Jesus used her as example to say her drive to pursue wisdom and knowledge from across the known world will put those with lazy faith to shame?

She stepped out and changed her nation for the better. You know the story by now. God did it for her. He's doing it for me. And he will do it for you. See you next chapter. We've started the journey of building legacy…

Legacy Challenge 2

Create a manifesto of the affirmations and confessions from the last two chapters. See the '5 Steps To Create A Manifesto' in the last chapter or the action guide section. Start with the Affirmations Fit For A Queen section. Need more go to Chapter One in the YOU Are A Shining Star section. Also, if not already visit Earma at the WOW! Women website for additional scripture based affirmations. http://www.wowontheweb.com

It's in the receiving now. The Holy Ghost has already been sent. Salvation has come. Healing has already been paid for. What about prosperity? It's paid for too. So, get ready to receive by faith whatever you need. Your family, your house and your work is blessed because of YOUR seeds of service in God's Kingdom!

Chapter Three

Breaking the Generational Curse

A Woman's War Using Words

Do you not understand that everything that goes into the mouth passes into the stomach, and is eliminated? But the things that proceed out of the mouth come from the heart, and those defile the man. For out of the heart come evil thoughts, murders, adulteries, fornications, thefts, false witness, slanders....—Matthew 15:17,18

Queen Jezebel distinguished herself in creating an evil legacy for Israel. The people trembled at the mention of her name. Under her rule, 850 of the palace prophets were executed in a battle of the gods hosted and led by Prophet Elijah.

Her decrees sent the prophets in the land into hiding. What power did she weld that all Christians do well to avoid? Her name, her life and evil actions still symbolize the spirit of control and the sin of rebellion against God today.

It's a known fact, Queen Jezebel had a strong gift of influence, as most women do. Yet, her strong power to influence went beyond normal; it overflowed into an evil spirit of control, never taking no as an answer.

History records her gifts and talents were extraordinary but for evil. What a different story we could be telling, if she had only learned how to stir up her husband and children to love God and good works. (2 Timothy 1:6; 2 Peter 1:13).

Her misdirected gifs of influence and talents, instead, brought upon her a curse. Even though, the evil she perpetrated was done under the guise of religion, it was nothing like what Father God says true religion looks like.

The Apostle James wrote, "Pure, undefiled religion, according to God our Father, is to take care of orphans and widows when they suffer and to remain uncorrupted by this world. - James 1:27

Beginning A Legacy

A Woman's War Using Words

Above all else, guard your heart, for everything you do flows from it. — Proverbs 4:23

Queen Jezebel welded her words for evil in a powerful way. Her legacy is the epitome of what we don't want to be like. Whenever her decrees went forth, the people and especially the prophets went into hiding.

Although, most of us are still learning our authority as queens we still have power in our words to be responsible for in our modern day. No one is exempt. We are made in the image of God, therefore we all have that creative power in our tongue and ultimately our words.

Have you ever said something, you wished you hadn't said? Not long ago, I wrote words on social media post that sounded all right at the time to the women I encourage at WOW Women Global. Later, the Holy Spirit prompted (convicted) me that it was too harsh and too direct. I remembered the words of a past leader, it's better that we err on the side of mercy.

As for the post, I ended up deleting it; not because the words were not true. But because it lacked the gracious tone it needed. I rewrote it with grace sprinkled heavily. I can hear some of you saying, you're just mercy motivated, Earma, everyone is not like that.

I can agree; everyone is not like that. I can only say, Jesus is like that, mercy motivated. I could go to many different passages. But remember, when right after he received the news about his cousin John's beheading he pulled aside to go up the mountain alone, probably to grieve.

But the people spotted him, gathered all their sick and vexed to bring to him. He saw them, instead of saying, "Can't a man have a moment alone? Instead the word of God says he saw them and was moved with compassion. He healed and delivered them ALL.

Furthermore, the Holy Spirit is not like that. He is gentle and compassionate in nature. He convicts us of sin but is gentle in restoration. He woos us even when we don't deserve his wooing. He's constantly drawing us near and drawing us back to God. He's pointing to and revealing Jesus, causing us to remember his words.

Back to my point, I've noticed that it's God's way that we be very careful with our words. You might be asking, why? For one thing, it really is true that the power of life and death resides in the tongue, your mouth. Couple that with the fact our words put a deposit in our hearts that the issues of life flow from.

So, whether we believe it or not, each day we are depositing in our heart with the words we speak, whether for good or evil. In light of that, think for a moment about the deposit that you are making. Is it doubt, fear, unbelief, doom and yes even death and cursing?

Secondly, the words we speak have power. Besides, making the deposit I spoke of earlier, they have the power to influence our own mind and heart (We believe what we say. We listen to our OWN voice more than anyone else) and the hearts of others.

Don't believe me yet, let's examine some things Jesus and a few others said that support and align with the importance of our words.

The religious leaders of that day were always testing Jesus and trying to prove him wrong in some way or trip him up in his words. So, in rebuking them he said, "You brood of vipers, how can you who are evil say anything good? For [we all know] the mouth speaks what the heart is full of."

Then again later, Jesus was instructing the disciples about a story he had just told, "It's not what you take in or eat that defiles a man. It's what comes out of you from your heart that defiles you. For murders, adulteries, and all manner of sin all come from the heart."

This is why the proverbial writer instructed us to, "Guard your heart for out of it flows the issues of life."

One more, the Apostle James warned us with, "The tongue also is a fire, a world of evil among the parts of the body. It corrupts the whole body, sets the whole course of one's life on fire, and is itself set on fire by hell."

By now, I'm pretty sure you've gotten my point. Be careful with your words. Take a minute and examine what is coming out of your mouth and heart. Are they good words of life, encouragement and faith building? I mean, are you speaking the word of God over your life, family and ministry?

I say all this because, at the time of this writing, Easter is almost here, when we commemorate our Lord's death, burial and resurrection. He paid a great and horrible price for our life more abundantly. It would be a sore disrespect to receive such a great gift, the grace of God and tear it all away with our words.

I've been working on keeping a tight rein on my words, maybe you have too. But I've discovered it's not always easy to do...

So, won't you join me in setting a guard over our mouth that our words might be holy before God more and more? My prayer is that we speak blessings and life over our life and the lives that surround us. Let it be so much so, that when we speak blessing it would actually mean something with the power to change the world for the good and bring glory to His name. May God bless you and make his face shine upon you, your family and ministry.

Building A Legacy

The Power Of Life And Death Are In Your Words

I call heaven and earth to record this day, that I have set before you life and death, blessing and cursing: therefore choose life, that both you and your children may live —Deuteronomy 30:19 para.

Queen Jezebel left an evil legacy of conspiracy, theft, murder and the spirit of control that led to a curse on her life and her children. She was the daughter of Ethbaal, king of the Zidonians, both king and priest of Baal worshipers. The Phoenicians were said to be a remarkable race, and outstanding as the great maritime peoples of the ancient world. But they were idolaters who regarded Jehovah as only a local deity, "the god of the land."

Their gods were Baal and Ashtaroth or Astarte, with their innumerable number of priests, 450 of whom Ahab installed in the magnificent temple to the Sun-god he had built in Samaria.

Another 400 priests were housed in a sanctuary Jezebel erected for them, and which she fed at her own table. Cruel and licentious rites were associated with the worship of Baal.

Jezebel sprang from an idolatrous stock, the same source which afterward produced the greatest soldier of antiquity, Hannibal, whose temper was not more daring and unforgiving than hers.

It was this heathen woman who married Ahab, king of Northern Israel, and who in so doing was guilty of a rash and impious act which resulted in evil consequences. As a Jew, Ahab sinned against his Hebrew faith in taking as his wife the daughter of a man whose very name, Ethbaal, meant, "A Man of Baal."

So, let's discuss our words and the effect it has on our lives. Every day, we are speaking our life forth. Now, let's make sure we are making good choices.

Stick And Stones May Hurt My Bones But Words Will Never Hurt Me

How many times have we said, it was just words? 'Sticks and stones may break my bones but words will never hurt me.' It's just not true. I heard the same child's chant growing up. I even tried to repeat it to myself when someone said something mean that really hurt. Especially, when I didn't want it to. And I wanted even less to show it.

Well, I think you get my point. The truth is there's power of life and death in our words. In fact, words are a serious matter. I'll prove it to you scripturally, in a moment. Then before I end, I have to tell you about the strange and wonderful purpose God has for us and our words.

Before those scriptures, let me tell you about a dear girlfriend. It seems like forever now; the Holy Spirit has been strict with me about my words. I used to work in corporate banking for years before I became an Authorpreneur. During those years, I worked for a bank that failed and laid everyone off in a couple of years. I was the new girl in the office of about twenty. Before me, this young lady from India used to be the new girl.

My first day, she started blaming things on me. Any mistake in the paperwork, any office equipment that was left on, I got blamed for it.

Finally, I had enough. I went directly to her and said in a couple of sentences to quit it. I was not the one to treat like that. Well, long story short, she ran off to our supervisor's office, screaming like I had slapped her and said I cursed her out.

Our supervisor came out walking toward me with a stern face, leaving her still crying and hiccupping that I was most rude and cursed her out. The supervisor said to me, "Earma, I was really surprised that you would do such a thing. We all know how religious and God-fearing you are."

To my amazement, I told her exactly what I said and asked her to ask the young lady what exact curse words I used. She chuckled saying, no she didn't quite describe it like that and went back in her office. I never heard anything else about it.

But later, I prayed about it. I asked the Holy Spirit why the young lady reacted in such a strong manner to my seemingly simple words. His immediate response, "Your words have authority and power."

Our Personal Words Have Power

My journey began with the Holy Spirit teaching me about the power of not only words, in general, but OUR PERSONAL WORDS and the Bible, God's words. By the way, the young lady and I became very good friends. God graced me to lead her to Christ before our jobs expired.

That was the season, God began teaching me about the need we all have to re-program our words, our minds and align them with the word of God more and more. Actually, in the Bible it's called renewing our mind with the word of God. Along with that, came the power to break old habits.

I would go on word fasts. You know refraining from things like gossip, criticism, complaints, and evil spoken words (disagreement with God's word about myself and others he had called me to pray for and speak truth over.)

Don't get me wrong, I didn't think this up on my own. It's how the Holy Spirit led me. If not already, he wants to do the same with you. Stay with me now, there's purpose in all this word changing and shaping...

One of the first people, He led me to with a wonderful God given revelation on the power of words was Charles Capps. Father God supernaturally, started talking to me about this man of God. New in the faith, I had never heard of him.

If you live in Dallas, you may remember this bill board for the Capps Truck and Van Rental. I would drive by this billboard on the way to work and on the way from work. Every day, for a few months, I would look over at the billboard Capps Rental and would sense the Spirit of God.

I finally asked my husband, do you know anyone by the name of Capps? God keeps talking to me about him but I don't know what it's about. He said, 'Yeah, I know Charles Capps!

I remember him always saying to our congregation at Agape Church, "I came all the way from England to be with you! England, Arkansas, that is. Everyone would laugh, then he would teach. He's a great teacher. I can't believe you don't know anything about him.

I began to get excited and wanted to know what his main teaching was. I remember holding my breath in anticipation. I knew it was an important next principle to learn in my faith journey. He said, I don't remember but he's famous for teaching the principle 'Calling things that are not as though they were.' I ordered his book the next day and the rest is history.

I now read this book afresh annually. It revolutionized my life and thinking about my words and the word of God. I recommend you read it, too. If you haven't read it already, it's *The Tongue, A Creative Force* by Charles Capps. You'll going to love it. Well, I recommend after you finish reading this book to read his as additional reading to build your faith in this area. Now, for those scriptures:

1. We are imitators of our Father God in this speaking... First of all, we can notice God spoke the world into existence in Genesis 1. God said, Let there be light, the rest of the universe and it was.

2. We all have power in our words... The tongue has the power of life and death, and those who love it will eat its fruit. —Proverbs 18:21

3. We displease God when we criticize our leaders and authorities. In fact, He gets pretty upset when we bad mouth our leaders...Remember, Miriam and Aaron. ...Not so, with My servant Moses, He is faithful in all My household.

With him I speak mouth to mouth, even openly, and not in dark sayings, and he beholds the form of the LORD. Why then were you not afraid to speak against My servant, against Moses?" —Numbers 12:7,8

4. We can transfer a bad attitude to the whole team with our words. If you get full of words of doubt, unbelief and criticism and talk to your fellow team members, there it goes, the spread of a bad attitude. By the way, it works the same way with passing a good attitude, too.

So, watch your attitude. It can be passed like the common cold, good or bad... as those who have been chosen of God, holy and beloved, put on a heart of compassion, kindness, humility, gentleness and patience; — Colossians 3:12

5. We can start a fire in our lives and the lives of others with the wrong words. The Apostle James warned us with, "The tongue also is a fire, a world of evil among the parts of the body. It corrupts the whole body, sets the whole course of one's life on fire, and is itself set on fire by hell."

6. Nonetheless, we can bless and speak right words over ourselves, our family and the world beyond. You can cooperate with the Holy Spirit so much so that God can begin to order the angels through your words. You can begin to express your desire and see good things come to pass in the world because God can trust your words.

In fact, it's God's purpose to use our words to change the world for better. Agree with what God says about the matter and you'll find the power of God activates. And Samuel grew, and the LORD was with him, and did let none of his words fall to the ground. —1 Samuel 3:19

By now, I'm pretty sure you've gotten my point. Be careful with your words. Take a minute and examine what's coming out of your mouth and heart. For the words that are coming out of your mouth are being deposited into your heart, thereby shaping your future, even your destiny.

Are they good words of life, encouragement and faith building? I mean, are you speaking the word of God over your life, family, team and ministry? Are you renewing your mind with the word of God and growing in power with God?

If so, great keep speaking your good words. Pretty soon, you'll begin to see the fruit of them come to pass more and more. If not, now is the time to change the tide. Allow the Holy Spirit to change your bad or slack words to a river of clear, clean words of life for all to enjoy. In doing so, change your life and world forever. Won't you join me in transforming your life by renewing your words daily? God bless you.

Strengthening Your Legacy

Breaking The Generational Curse And Sealing The Blessing

For if ye be Christ's, then ye are Abraham's Seed and heirs according to the promises. Galatians 3:29

God has the plan of blessings for each generation, that the **blessing** might multiply. Remember, his plan is for our good, a happy ending, a bright future for each family and person.

But, none of the blessings work automatic, even though they belong to us. They become manifested in our lives as we exercise our faith to receive them.

The force of faith must be applied by the word of God in your heart and by the confession of your mouth. —Romans 8:11 For if ye be Christ's, then ye are Abraham's Seed and heirs according to the promises. —Galatians 3:29 More about this later.

To expand our understanding, the meaning of establish is to make steadfast, firm or stable; to settle on a firm (foundation) or permanent basis; the set or fix unalterably. God has set or fixed this covenant with you and me in our day to such a degree that the promise cannot be altered. The promises of God are guaranteed by God. No power can alter God's covenant with you.

So, the New Covenant, ratified in the blood of Jesus was the fulfillment of God's promise to Abraham. It is a better covenant than came through Moses, and it rests upon better promises —Hebrews 8:6 The Old Covenant was incomplete as far as man's needs were concerned. It could not change men's hearts; it could only bless them physically and materially —Galatians 3:21; Galatians 3:13,14,26,29

The word of God proclaims Christ hath redeemed us from the curse of the law, being made a curse for us...That the blessing of Abraham might come on the Gentiles through Jesus Christ; that we might receive the promise of the Spirit through faith...For ye are all the children of God by faith in Christ Jesus...And if ye be Christ's then are ye Abraham's seed, and heirs according to the promise.

The Generational Curse

We, now, can recognize the curse started with consequences or results of disobedience to God in the Garden. Adam, Eve and the Serpent each received judgement from Father God for their part in the disobedience. Therefore, each birth since then was born subject to a sinful nature and to the awful curse. –Genesis 1

For example, have you ever noticed a family, seemingly, bent toward a certain sin or vice. We can all point to a family's struggle with things like alcoholism, infidelity and divorce. Each generation that succumbs to sin, the bent becomes stronger and stronger. You may hear people whisper; it seems as if a curse is on their family. The generations are marked with suicides, fatal accidents, sudden deaths, or slow death from disease.

Then there are other families who struggle with an extraordinary number of members that struggle with poverty, homelessness, high school dropouts, teen pregnancy, abortion and promiscuousness? Hang in there with me, I promise there's a good news message coming.

On the other hand, you may notice another family, where generation after generation the blessing seems to increase until they are known for their wealth and distinguished for their accomplishments. Their family includes a long list of doctors, lawyers, educators, bankers, millionaires and wealthy family members. It becomes obvious, the blessing of the Lord is on the family.

Here's another thing I've noticed, most universities and hospitals were started by Christians who know God and have tapped into the blessing of God. For most, you can trace the founding of the university or hospital back to an obedient believer who had a revelation about the blessing. Which brings me to my point of this chapter, to break the generational curse the first step is to gain knowledge about the curse and then get acquainted with God's blessing.

Even, change your inner image from poverty to prosperity, from sickness to health, no purpose to destiny and from hopelessness to faith. Here in lies the good news of the Gospel of Jesus Christ.

So, keep going with me. We'll discuss how to de-activate the curse. And we're going to get acquainted with the blessing of God. We study how you can receive it, experience it, walk in it and then pass it to your children and children's children.

If your family is experiencing all of what I mentioned earlier, this can change with a revelation of God's blessing. The blessing that has already been purchased for you through the transaction of heaven over 2000 years ago. It's the blessing that God purchased with the blood of Christ with his death, burial and resurrection.

The Propitiation – Jesus Our Substitute

To lay a good foundation, let's discuss Jesus, our substitute. When wrongs are committed, retribution and justice are demanded. Mercy is applied. There is one and only one reason, all sufficient reason for God's mercy. The **propitiation**, *the substitute* given while we were yet sinners and still sinning. The substitute was supplied through a transaction of heaven. Jesus' blood was applied to the mercy seat in heaven.

Remember when Mary of Magdalene, inadvertently interrupted Jesus on his way to settle it once and for all. He was on the way to appear in heaven at the mercy seat of God to pay the ultimate price, the ultimate sacrifice, His life for ours. His Blood for our freedom.

Therefore, we can say, Jesus was punished, yet without sin, so we could be forgiven. Jesus was wounded that we might be healed. He was made sin with our sinfulness that we might be free from the curse of the law and sin. He paid the price with his blood, so we might be free from the curse of sickness, the curse of poverty and any other effects of sin.

Sooooo, the good news is, it's already given to us. Now, it's all in the receiving. If your family is immersed in the effects of the curse, then this is for you. And even if your family's previous generations have received the blessing but somehow you're seeing it slip away in your generation, this is for you, too.

Breaking The Generational Curse

Wherever you are in your Christian walk, you can begin to reverse the curse. You may know by now, people perish for lack of knowledge, when they simply don't know any better. Our enemy the devil seeks to make sure you don't know or find out so that generation after generation, he can run rampant over you and your family.

So, if you begin to get some resistance or a ruckus is started, persevere. Keep reading; keep getting knowledge. God will make sure you arrive safely in his kingdom. Because, our enemy knows if you can get one word of revelation, your life will change and all of those you influence.

With that said, you could say people are blessed and prosper with knowledge. There's a scripture that I pray almost daily, "Father thank you that you are a sure foundation for every circumstance or problem I face. You are a rich store of salvation, wisdom and knowledge for me. I use the key to this treasure. I reverence you and draw out all that I need."

There are volumes of books written on this subject of breaking the curse. So, I didn't try to write everything in this chapter. But, I do hope I went far enough and deep enough, so you can begin to break the curse and activate the blessing in your life.

And not only that, but become a blessing to your children's children and others that are in your circle of influence. Here are seven steps that will get you started breaking the generational curse against your family and activating the blessing of God:

Get knowledge from the word of God about the curse and the blessing. I'm not saying we should immerse ourselves in studying the curse. I am saying we should lay a correct foundation from the word of God and know about the curse and its effect. Most of us were perishing from lack of knowledge in this area.

Then study the blessing. Read the Bible and other Christian teaching. Listen to preaching on it. This book is a good start. I recommend Bill Winston and many others. Then meditate on the blessing scriptures. Here's a good one to start with: The blessing of the Lord maketh rich and he adds no trouble to it. −Proverbs 10:22

Pray the prayer of release to align your life with God to break the curse. Before praying the Prayer Of Release, you should familiarize yourself with four main areas that many overlook. Through lack of knowledge or unbelief, they mistakenly think it has nothing to do with the effects of the curse in their life and ultimately the blessing of God: repent - revoke – replace.

Cancel every evil word spoken against your business, your ministry and ability to prosper; cancel negative confessions about yourself; then, acknowledge Christ and pray the prayer of release. (See the Action Guide section for full Prayer of Release.)

Get acquainted with the blessing of God, already on your life as a Christian. Did you know Father God blessed you beyond your wildest dreams, ALREADY? Most of us know, God chose us from the foundations of the world. So, if he chose us back then, when did he bless us? He blessed us before the foundations of the world. Realize the more you find out about God's blessing, the more your faith increases. And the more your faith increases, the less you will put up with, the works of the devil and the curse. You'll rise up and say, my Lord paid for that, so I don't have to put up with lack, poverty, not being able to focus on my destiny...

Change your inner image by meditating the word of God. If you chronically deal with poverty, you may have an inner image of being poor. Or you might be at the point, Joshua and the Israelites were when they stood on the banks of the Jordan River facing the walls of Jericho. God told Joshua the secret key to success and walking in your destiny, "Never stop reciting these teachings.

You must think about them night and day so that you will faithfully do everything written in them. Only then will you prosper and succeed." – Joshua 1 (Need help on meditating on the promises of God? See Action Guide section with '7 Steps To MEDITATE The Word Of God.'

Appropriate the blessing. Begin to apply the blessing to your life and those you pray and speak the word of God over. Personalize and meditate on the blessing of God. Again, a good scripture to start with is: The blessing of the Lord brings wealth and adds no trouble to it. -Proverbs 10:22 I know, I know I quoted the same scripture. Some things are just worth repeating. See the section below for additional scriptures and affirmations to use.

Speak the Blessing. As you meditate more and more, the right image grows inside you. Begin to speak the word of God, and it will begin to bear fruit in your life.

Be the Blessing. After you learn about the curse, study the blessing, pray the prayer to break any curses, change your inner image and start speaking the blessing, you will start being a blessing, more and more.

∽∾

A Legacy Of Blessing

The Power Of Words To Bless

God is sovereign, meaning he's in charge. So, I can say, it's by faith and revelation that we receive this abundant provision of mercy, the blessing. God, sovereignly, ordains and orders that we receive each provision. He discerns the motives and even the state of our heart. So, when we approach the throne boldly on the basis of Christ's sacrifice, we still need to be sensitive to the leading of the Holy Spirit.

Allow Father God to save in the order, he chooses and sees fit. For example, most of us want to receive the prosperity part of the blessing first but God may want us to focus on receiving His righteousness, his sanctification and then his prosperity. Or he may want to heal us before we can receive forgiveness. If we stubbornly claim and ask for we want or think is right we may not receive either.

With that said, the Scripture says the tongue has the power of life and death. Words play an important role in conveying the blessing. When Israel blessed Manasseh and Ephraim, he laid his hands on their heads and boldly said, "By you Israel will bless, saying, 'May God make you as Ephraim and as Manasseh.'" (Genesis 48:20)

Our words create labels that may last a lifetime. We can express acceptance and love or rejection and disapproval. Physiologists confirm it takes ninety-nine positive words to eliminate the effect of one negative word or phrase. It took me a long time to turn the tide of negative words coming out of my mouth in my own life. It seemed even longer to realize the definite power my words have on other people for good or detriment.

I am beginning to realize that often Father God is looking for someone to agree (believe) with him in fulfilling his promises in our lives. Join me in making the decision I made years ago to begin to agree with God. Starting with the small; not only for our life but for those in our family and others God will begin to put in your path.

For example, a rebellious friend of the family would curse, swear, gossip incessantly. If anyone even mentioned the word prayer, she would get upset and refuse prayer. Our family had for years unknowingly agreed with Satan saying she's always going to be like that. She's never going to come to God. She was born with a contrary streak.

Why do you think she's going to change now? But God begin to whisper to me, "She's an influencer when she comes to Me, many will follow. I want to save her and all those she influences. I want to change her heart and grant her health and peace in abundance."

Not long after, I would discover myself saying the same things my family would say and stop in mid-sentence. I began to agree with God. I would say what I heard Him say.

I am continuing to see change after change take place in her life. Her heart is softened more and more. I haven't seen a complete change but I haven't given up. Why? Because God hasn't given up; he still whispers about His desires for her. Who is God calling you to agree with Him about?

Speaking God's Blessings Over Your Life

In earlier chapters, we learned that we are responsible for filling up the depository of our heart and guarding it for the issues (our destiny) flows out of it. I've inserted some more ammunition here to renew your mind with the Word of God. Continue with these blessings and then more I believes:

1. I am blessed when I come in and blessed when I go out. Deuteronomy 28
2. Father, I speak a blessing over _____. May it run after them and overtake them. –Deuteronomy 28
3. I trust in the Lord my God so I am blessed.
4. Father thank you for blessing me with favor and honor that encompasses me about as a shield.
5. The Lord's blessing brings wealth and he adds no trouble to it. Proverbs 10:22
6. God says he has a good plan for my life in Jeremiahs 29:11. I am going to fulfill my destiny and be all that I can be for His glory. God gave me gifts and talents, and I intend to use them to help others.
7. I am nothing, and yet I am everything! In myself I am nothing, and yet in Jesus I am everything I need to be. –John 15:5

Realize the power of blessing through YOUR words can change a life and a lifetime of ill-spoken words. Stay humble, be patient and watch your faith-filled words of life and blessings construct a new life for you, your family and those God has called you to influence.

Legacy Snippet

Setting A Watch Over Our Words

May my prayer be counted as incense before You; The lifting up of my hands as the evening offering. Set a guard, O LORD, over my mouth; Keep watch over the door of my lips. Do not incline my heart to any evil thing, to practice deeds of wickedness With men who do iniquity; And do not let me eat of their delicacies. —Psalm 141:2,3,4

On my first job, I learned a deep lesson that I never forgot. I had just turned sixteen and excited to work on my first public job. My father had shown me some side streets to drive on to get there. I didn't have to go on any main streets, if I didn't want to.

Of course, after getting to know a few of the ladies in the office and overhearing them talking about their great deals that they got. Well, to get access to those stores and those deals, I had to drive there. So, I took up my courage and drove there.

One afternoon, I got back from lunch and the office was in an uproar. One of the older (to me) ladies in the office, Johnnie, was crying and inconsolably. According to her, just the day before she got in an altercation with one of the supervisors in the office.

She stormed away and said, "I hope you drop dead!" She found that he did, later that evening. He literally dropped dead. I know it's an extreme example. But it brings the spotlight over to how much our words affect our lives and even our destiny. It brings me to a question, I have for you.

Why do so many of us remember—in detail—all the negative words our family said, from when we became aware at four or five until today? "You're never going to amount to much." "This room is always a mess." "You never listen to me. That color will always look washed out on you. Will you ever stop growing? You're becoming a giant!"

Why can't a bike, a coveted Barbie doll or a ticket to your favorite concert make up for several things that hurt your feelings? Why do we remember criticism more than positive ones? You can blame it on the brain. It's the way, our brains are wired.

Studies by Dr. John Cacioppo of the University of Chicago have shown what he calls "the negativity bias" of the brain. Our brains are naturally more sensitive and responsive to unpleasant news. That's why personal insults or criticism hit us hard and stay with us longer. It's why negative ads, articles, reviews, TV shows grab out attention faster than positive ones—political or otherwise.

Dr. John Cacioppo's studies show the ratio for family is five to one. It takes about five positive comments to offset one negative comment. Other studies show the ratio even higher. Some say the ratio is even higher for strong energy words. These studies say the ratio is, it takes ten positive comments to offset one negative with strong energy words.

With all that said, do you truly want to walk in your destiny? Then watching your words and building a right image within yourself is a must.

First there's the rooting out of the weeds, the evil words. What are evil words, you might ask. Evil words are any words contrary to the word of God for yourself and others. Most of us, already know how much our words affect others. Again, scientific research explains that it takes ten positive comments to offset just one negative comment.

Years ago I received another faith project similar to the family member I mentioned earlier. This time, a close friend of mine was acting the way she always acted. Everyone that knew her would say, you know her she always does that and she always will. I must confess; I was agreeing with them. Yes, me with my campaign of getting my words in line. In my defense (smile), back then I thought it only applied to what I said about myself.

The Holy Spirit abruptly interrupted that thought. He explained, because of the light that I am, it also applies to what I say about other people. He impressed upon me the fact that I had to begin to agree with what God said about her.

It went against the grain of what everyone had been saying and believed about her, including herself. At that point, she probably didn't believe any differently than what had always been.

I started agreeing with what God said about her. Even when others said what they had always said and she did what she always did. I stayed in agreement with God said. I saw no change at first. Then, I began to see change for the better in my friend.

She began to say, I used to think I would never change but I'm changing. I used to never think this way but now I feel different. I feel like there's hope, even for me. It was all I could do to keep my composure. For sure, my spirit man ran all around that room. I'm still agreeing with God about her; before you know it she'll be a new person...

In another instance, I was talking with a friend about a mutual acquaintance. She said something negative about her, what she didn't like. I added my two cents about what I didn't like and what she had done to me that was truly bad. The conversation went back and forth a few minutes and then I left the room. Away from her, I whispered a prayer and repented because my Lord had taught me better.

I went back to my friend and said, "I'm sorry, even if it's true. I can't talk that way about her. I had to repent because the Holy Spirit convicted me that it was wrong."

Do you see it yet? Our words are closely connected to walking in our destiny. We have to rightly align our words to the word of God and his way.

Now, for building a right image within yourself with words. I've taught on this many times within the WOW! Women message and books. For more teaching on this topic, visit me at the WOW! Women website http://wowontheweb.com.

Remember, your destiny or future is stored up in your heart! It's not dictated by your past or your current circumstances. Actually, your destiny is decided by YOU. In the Scripture verse Matthew 12:34-35 paraphrased, "Out of the abundance of the heart the mouth speaks. A good woman out of the good treasure of the heart brings forth good things: and an evil woman out of her treasure brings forth evil things."

Jesus made this powerful point to explain that what was in your heart is what comes out. Have you wondered: Who stored up the evil things in the evil woman's heart? Clearly, the evil woman herself did. Who stored up the good things in the good woman's heart. Again, the woman herself did.

In the same way, we are the only ones that can store and harvest the Word of God in our heart. Our parents can't store good in our hearts. Neither can our spouse. Your godly leaders can't do it. Even God can't do it for us. In fact, Father God has already done His part to help us.

He's the One Who made our heart a depository for His Word. He opened an account for us when we were first born. Our heart remains a depository whether it is for good or bad. We will use our faith for the good or for the bad through the power of choice.

The writer of Romans says, "God has dealt to every man the measure of faith." (Romans 12:3) The moment each of us made a decision to receive Christ, God put an initial measure of faith in our heart. Yet, we are the only ones that can increase that store.

We can increase our deposit of faith by taking the Word of God and putting it into our heart. Each time, we make a deposit of God's Word, our faith balance grows and our future and destiny get brighter. The more we deposit, the better things are, because that is where we will draw from to change the circumstances in our life.

Our heart holds the faith we'll need to combat any negative circumstances the devil sends our way. It doesn't matter if he tries to put sickness, rejection or troubles in our life to predict our end. We can draw from the Word of God about healing, acceptance or deliverance and it will give us victory in that area.

Won't you join me in faith and let's set a watch over our mouth and our words to the glory of God. We acknowledge without God's help; we can't change or speak the way we should. We commit our conversation to you, Lord. Help us speak the right words and order our conversation the way we should.

Summing It All Up

Did you get started breaking generational curses and sealing the blessing in your life? I re-discovered this topic is heavy but needful. Because of lack of knowledge, like me, you may have a tide of wrong words to turn.

Be patient with waiting for the Lord to act. It takes time to change the tide. Keep working out your salvation, meditating the word of God, speaking the word of God and agreeing with God. It will change.

I was somber to realize Queen Jezebel had a strong gift of influence, as most women do. Yet, her strong power to influence went beyond normal; it overflowed into an evil spirit of control, never taking no as an answer. I hope you remember, as I did, we women all have a gift of influence and power in our words to be responsible for.

History records Queen J gifts and talents were extraordinary but for evil. What a different story we could be telling, if she had only learned how to stir up her husband and children to love God and good works. Remember, we are writing our own story with words. I encourage you to write it well. For it surely will be told.

See you next chapter, we discuss 'Overcoming The Giants Of Your Generation'. We're still on the journey of building legacy…

Legacy Challenge 3

Apply the word of God: Go on a word fast. For example, start a two-day fast of no complaints. If you even start a complaint, you must replace it with a compliment or a grateful statement about the same thing. To hold yourself accountable, tell a friend what you are doing or make a post on Facebook. Next time, do it for a week. Let us know at http://wowontheweb.com under testimonials how it went.

Chapter Four

Overcoming the Giants Of Your Generation

A Woman's Will To Win

So the LORD gave Israel all the land he had sworn to give their ancestors, and they took possession of it and settled there. -—Joshua 21:43

*D*avid and Goliath are two of the most famous men in the Bible. Then there's that famous battle which is probably a close second in notoriety. But did you know two important and distinguished women are in the family tree of these men? The two women are Ruth and Orpah, daughters-in-law of Naomi.

In fact, Ruth and Orpah are famous for their respective decisions. These decisions are at the heart of the gospel of Jesus Christ. Naomi was leaving Moab to return to her home town.

She had suffered great loss in a foreign land, they resided in to escape the famine. Interestingly, she eventually experienced a greater personal famine in Moab, when she lost her two sons and her husband.

She lamented that she left full but was returning empty. Out of concern for her two daughters-in-law, she urged them both to return to their families. She explained they would have a better chance to marry again and receive new husbands in their own homeland than staying with her a devastated widow in old age. She urgently pushed them to return, for it was not like she would have any more sons to grow up and marry them.

Orpah decided to take her mother-in-law's advice. She returned to her family. Jewish history, records she became the matriarch of the family of giants that Goliath descended from. She met her demise at the hands of Abishai, mighty man and captain in King David's army. That's another story for another time.

On the other hand, Ruth, the former Moabite priestess, would not leave Naomi's side. Under oath, she promised to let her family become hers and not only that but let Naomi's God become her god.

Beginning A Legacy

The Choice Of Hope

Look, today I am giving you the choice between a blessing and a curse! — Deuteronomy 11:26

There are strategic times in life and even crossroads, like Ruth and Orpah when we have to make a decision whether we will go back or move forward in faith. It was at such a time, my good friend and I were going back and forth, over and over again trying to come up with a solution for my problem.

After more than several times, my friend said out loud what she had probably been thinking all along, "It's hopeless. You have no choice but to give up!"

Suddenly, my faith rose up in me. The word of God that I had been storing up, for quite some time by then, burst forth and I said, "There's always a choice. It's not hopeless. We serve a God of miracles. There's always a choice. We can choose hope or give up. I choose hope.

Father God is going to work this out for me. I don't know how but He's going to do something. A few minutes later, the phone rang. The person on the other end was a part of the solution, God sent. I didn't know it. But I had just preached my first message on hope and expectation, to my friend and myself.

Now I can add to that. Father God gave humanity back in the Garden of Eden, starting with Adam, the power of choice. You see, he didn't want robots. If he had just put a computer chip, so to speak, of obedience inside us, there would be no relationship.

Instead, he gave us the power to choose. All of us, in humanity have this power. Even though through Adam and Eve, we broke God's heart and chose to disobey, forfeiting our rights to Satan.

For the word of God says, Therefore, just as through one-man sin entered into the world, and death through sin, and so death spread to all men, because all sinned —Romans 5:12 We could say through one man's choice, Adam, representative of humanity, sin and death entered the world.

But through another man's choice, Jesus, Savior of the world, righteousness and life re-entered the world. Through our Lord's choice in the Garden of Gethsemane, the second Adam, made the choice of not my will, but your will Father, not my way but your way Father...

It's still a mystery to us, how a death could redeem the opportunity to choose. But it did, hallelujah! Of course, it wasn't just any death. It was the death of our Lord, the Christ. Another place, his choice was evident was when in response to his critics Jesus responded as the Good Shepherd, "For this reason the Father loves Me, because I lay down My life so that I may take it again.

"No one has taken it away from Me, but I lay it down on My own initiative (choice). I have authority to lay it down, and I have authority to take it up again. This commandment I received from My Father." —John 10:17,18

Do you see it, yet? In other words, he said it's Father God's way. He gave me the choice. I chose his way. I chose to lay my life down. No one took it from me.

It is also written, "The first MAN, Adam, BECAME A LIVING SOUL." The last Adam became a life-giving spirit.

By God's Grace, the opportunity has been granted again. We can choose life more abundantly through choosing Christ. We have been predestined through Christ to live a life devoted to God.

Again, in other words, to walk in our destiny our first choice is Christ. Then we choose to submit to him as Lord, the same decision Christ made in the Garden of Gethsemane. You know, the 'Not my will, but your will Father – Not my way but your way.'

Today, we choose Christ. We choose life and the blessing. Therefore, we say afresh, it's our choice to live God's way and receive his destiny, his appointment and his blessing.

Building Your Legacy

The Conquest and the F.I.G.H.T. Principle

Then Caleb silenced the people before Moses and said, "We should go up and take possession of the land, for we can certainly do it." Numbers 13:30

Way before the day of Naomi, Ruth and Orpah there was another crossroads and decision being made that changed history and the destiny of the Israelites. Moses had led the Israelites, 100s of thousands of them out of Egypt the long way, as God instructed. He wanted to ready the people for what lay ahead.

It was a long awaited day, for the Israelites. They camped opposite the Promised Land territory, God had been telling them about for quite some time. Moses sent out twelve spies to see what the land was like. After forty days, the twelve assigned spies including Joshua and Caleb, came back with a report of what it was like in the Promised Land.

The mission was to gather facts to inspire and rally the people to go in and possess the land. Instead, through unbelief and doubt, ten of the spies came back with a bad report.

And it had the opposite effect on the congregation. It moved them to disbelief and criticism of Moses and Aaron. So much so, Father God was angry about it. Let's look in the word of God for a moment to see how the ten spies, Joshua and Caleb responded

We Can Do It!

When they returned from spying out the land, at the end of forty days, they came back to Moses and Aaron and the whole Israelite community at Kadesh in the Desert of Paran. There they reported to them and to the whole assembly and showed them the fruit of the land.

They gave Moses this account: "We went into the land to which you sent us, and it does flow with milk and honey! Here is its fruit. But the people who live there are powerful, and the cities are fortified and very large. We even saw descendants of Anak there. The Amalekites live in the Negev; the Hittites, Jebusites and Amorites live in the hill country; and the Canaanites live near the sea and along the Jordan." Then Caleb silenced the people before Moses and said,

"We should go up and take possession of the land, for we can certainly do it."

But the men who had gone up with him said, "We can't attack those people; they are stronger than we are." And they spread among the Israelites a bad report about the land they had explored. They said, "The land we explored devours those living in it. All the people we saw there are of great size. We saw the Nephilim there (the descendants of Anak come from the Nephilim). We seemed like grasshoppers in our own eyes, and we looked the same to them." —Numbers 13:25-31

In light of that story, are you possessing your land? You know as a Christian believer, God has promised you a type of Promised Land? It's the fulfillment of His promises to you in your life. And yes, this land is flowing with milk and honey.

The fruit is so bountiful that it takes two well-abled men to carry it. Remember, the cluster of grapes lifted on two poles depicted in all the Promised Land pictures from the story…

The power of your good life or your demise is your mouth. Your present and your future is built by what you say, your words. Therefore, it's all in your heart and hints of it in your life already. No one has to tell you what to need and want. It's dictated by the deposits of your words and impacted by the words of others. Your present world is built by the power, the source of your words up to this point.

So, if you want to change your future, your destiny, change your words. Re-word what you are saying on a daily basis. Remember, our warfare is not accomplished by natural means but it's mighty (God's way) to the pulling down of strongholds. Casting down every selfish imagination and replacing it with the Word of God. -2 Corinthians 10:4,5

The Conquest

Even with the beauty and potential of possessing our Promised Land in all its bigness and grandeur, there's one small matter we Christians share with the Israelites. We overlook the fact that we have to fight to possess this promised land and in our case the promises of God. We're alike in a lot of other ways with our Israelite brothers and sisters in God's family.

We have to face the same fears, insecurities and doubt, when we see the giants that stand in our way of possessing the promised land. Did you notice all the residents listed in Scripture were giants (We even saw descendants of Anak there?

The Amalekites live in the Negev; the Hittites, Jebusites and Amorites live in the hill country; and the Canaanites), many descendants from Goliath's relatives. Many scholars have said over the years, the giants the spies saw were perceived instead of literal, from them saying "we seemed like grasshoppers in our own eyes, and we looked the same to them."

Through study, archaeological digs, and Jewish history, the Biblical account has been confirmed, the Promised Land residents were literal giants. And no, as a believer I didn't need confirmation that the Bible is true. But I find it highly interesting and faith building to say the least. I hope you do too.

Your promised land may be a healthy life, a prosperous life or a blessed family. And the giants of sickness, lack, and family trouble are very real, as well. In fact, we have to make the same type of decision they had to make. We have to decide whose report will we believe? When the doctor's report comes in and it's bad. Or our money account has a few dollars left in it and we still have bills to pay. You might be in the middle of defeating the giant of divorce and alcoholism in your family.

For this book, WOW! Women of Legacy I studied for a chapter about defeating the giants in your generation. I did a study on the two women matriarchs Ruth and Orpah, respectively of David and the giant Goliath. I outlined seven steps, Father God gave me to defeat the giants of our generation. Here's a little acronym from that study called FIGHT to help us possess the promises of God in our lives more and more.

1. Face your fears with faith. You have to decide whose report to believe. When you face your fears and choose God's word to believe, you discover like never before God is for you, and who can really stand against you. More and more, you realize 'no weapon formed against you shall succeed and every accusation risen against you, you shall refute it.

Even, when other people have decided to believe a bad report, negative circumstances, we choose like Joshua and Caleb to believe the word of God. We believe, with God for us, we are well able to go up and take the land (receive the promise.)

2. Invite Father God's presence into your circumstance. So often, the last thing we think about is praying for his blessing or intervention. Make it your first step instead of our your last. Ask for his help, his mercy and grace or his miracle.

3. Grow up in the faith. Recognize you have to fight for the promises of God in your life. You can't stay a spiritual baby. You shouldn't have to go back and forth, always having to relearn the simple things of Christ. God's perfect will for us is that we grow up in the faith and fight for the things He's promised us.

This is the season for YOU to possess the promises of God in their fullness. But you have to be willing to grow up (man up and woman up) to fight the good fight of faith, God's way. Remember, our weapons of warfare are not carnal. The victory is already ours. Father God has said YES and amen to each of his promises

4. Hear Father God's Instruction. After you've prayed and you've asked for his miracle intervention, listen for God's guidance, his instructions. He may instruct you to ask, to fast, to plant a seed or wait for His next move. Yes, God's ways are mysterious but not unknowable.

Remember, get your plans, your strategies from God. He'll take you by the hand and help you. There are times you won't have to fight for the battle is the Lord's. There are other times where you must F.I.G.H.T. the good fight of faith, using weapons that are not carnal but mighty to the pulling down of strongholds. —2 Cor. 10:4

5. Take Territory for your life and the kingdom of God. It's all about territory. Father God wants to enlarge your territory bit by bit. It's so, you won't be overwhelmed and quit or lose. He will always set you up for success. But you have to live and fight God's way.

Know that each battle, you engage in, when you're victorious, you gain territory in the kingdom of God. You may be in the battle of your life, for your health, your finances, your home, your family...

On the other side, is your greatest victory and ministry. You've been chosen to show the way in this area. There's a group of people, a city, for some even a nation waiting on you to walk in your victory. So, you know what I'm about to say, F.I.G.H.T.

Yes, the promises are yes and amen, already. In Christ, we have the victory. But in possessing the land, receiving the promises, there has to be a conquest, a fight. Think about it, similar to a natural fight, you don't run out presumptuous, unprepared, imprudent and expect victory.

Instead, you execute wise planning, preparation and even training to prepare for the battle, the conquest, the victory. From my last teaching, T.R.U.S.T. you know that's what the process is all about, preparing you for the conquest.

In like manner, the Holy Spirit is prompting us the body of Christ to F.I.G.H.T. We have to face our fears, invite Father God's presence to go with us, grow up in the faith, hear Father God's instruction and gain territory in the kingdom of God.

So, you made it through the process, you did it God's way, your victory is sweet. But now it's time. You're ready. Get your gloves. Put your dukes up and F.I.G.H.T.

~

Strengthening Your Legacy

7 Steps To Defeat The Giants In Your Generation

This is the confidence which we have before Him, that, if we ask anything according to His will, He hears us. And if we know that He hears us in whatever we ask, we know that we have the requests which we have asked from Him. -1 John 5:14,15

Ruth was a surprise participate of the family blessing of Israel. Her new family rose up and blessed her and Boaz with their words, "Then the elders and all the people at the gate said, "We are witnesses. May the Lord make the woman who is coming into your home like Rachel and Leah, who together built up the family of Israel.

May you have standing in Ephrathah and be famous in Bethlehem. Through the offspring the Lord gives you by this young woman, may your family be like that of Perez, whom Tamar bore to Judah."

Naomi Gains a Son

So Boaz took Ruth and she became his wife. When he made love to her, the Lord enabled her to conceive, and she gave birth to a son. The women said to Naomi: "Praise be to the Lord, who this day has not left you without a guardian-redeemer.

May he become famous throughout Israel! He will renew your life and sustain you in your old age. For your daughter-in-law, who loves you and who is better to you than seven sons, has given him birth."

Then Naomi took the child in her arms and cared for him. The women living there said, "Naomi has a son!" And they named him Obed. He was the father of Jesse, the father of David.

> The Family Tree of David
> Perez was the father of Hezron,
> Hezron the father of Ram,
> Ram the father of Amminadab,
> Amminadab the father of Nahshon,
> Nahshon the father of Salmon,d
> Salmon the father of Boaz,
> Boaz the father of Obed,
> Obed the father of Jesse,
> and Jesse the father of David.

Life-changing decisions were made by the two women; we have been discussing in this chapter. Orpah went home and Ruth decided to follow Naomi and her God. Now, here's some family history, you may know already, Ruth went on to marry, Boaz, the Kinsman-Redeemer of her dead husband, Malhoh.

Boaz was the son of Salmon and Rahab. Then, Boaz and Ruth became the proud parents of Obed. Obed means a servant, a workman and a worshipper. Obed was the grandfather to King David. And on down the family tree, it went to Jesus, the firstborn of many in the faith.

Goliath represented a sinful generation, men and women without a covenant with God. David, on the other hand, was from a godly family and a man of covenant. He was in strong covenant with God and with men. His famous covenant with Jonathan, King Saul's son inspires us to this day.

Most princes headed for a kingship inheritance will knock off all threats, real or perceived. But not Jonathan, he loved and respected David so much, he exchanged vows with David. He declared he would be king, just as God had said through the Prophet Samuel.

Known as a man after God's own heart, books are written about David's character. Through his victory over Goliath, the chosen family progressed through the generations to the birth of the savior of mankind, Jesus Christ.

Because of Jesus, the Christ, his death, burial and resurrection, we as Christians have a covenant with God. Through the covenant with God, we are equipped for victory over any giant, hellacious obstacle and every mountain. Here's seven steps to overcome the giants of your generation.

1. Pinpoint the giant. Most of us, already know what the giant of our Promised Land is and where he is. Why, because, they are probably shouting the loudest, the most embolden. Either way, put the target on the giant for a change. The tables are about to switch. This thing has been shouting at your family for years, even generations.

2. Focus on one giant at a time. This one won't be hard. According to how big the giant is looming over your life, it may take all the focus you can muster. Even so, don't allow distraction to hinder you in getting the victory. This is surely one of the enemy's tactics. So many problems may crop up that you lose focus. If this happens, keep your eyes on the Lord. He will see you through. Don't give up. When it clears, start back and re-focus.

3. Pray and ASK for the victory. Rehearse the principles of ASKing in faith from WOW! Women of Destiny. Remember, asking is an activator of our faith. God wants us to ask and believe we receive, when we ask.

4. FIGHT God's way. Acknowledge it's not by your power or might but by the Spirit of the Lord. Ultimately, the battle is not yours, but the Lord's. In the name of the Lord, by the blood of the Lamb and the Word of God, you have the victory. He will show you which way to stand and fight the good fight of faith. Our weapons of warfare are not carnal but mighty to the pulling down of strongholds.

5. Get God's strategy. You've asked for the victory. You're ready to fight God's way. Now ask for God's wisdom and strategy. The word of God says, we can ask for wisdom. Father God will give it to us liberally, without finding any reason to hold back.

6. Receive it by faith. Now, faith is the substance of things hoped for. Receive the victory now; then act like it. Whatever you do when it manifests tangibly, do it now. Shout, jump around, clap, sing, testify. You get my point. It may not feel like you have the victory. But by faith, you do. Now, is a good time to shout amen!

7. Act on His instructions. Obey as quickly as you can. Timing is important. Opportunities, sometimes evaporate. So, whether you are instructed to fast, pray, raise your level of word intake, plant a seed, or all of the above, just do it. Then when you obey, continue to thank God for the victory. For if we ask anything according to the will of God, we know that he hears us. And if we know that he hears us then we have the petition that we have asked of him.

We thank God that all Scripture is God-breathed and inspired by him. It is useful for instruction and setting a great pattern that we can follow. Through the choice of hope Ruth made and the heart of repentance and obedience of her great-grandson King David, we are inspired to overcome the giants in our generation.

We can take up the five smooth stones of revelation and throw the Rock of Ages and hit our giant enemy right between the eyes. Then run up with the sword of the Spirit and chop his head off. Then shout for the victory is ours, even to our children's children! Hallelujah!

A Legacy of Reverence

11 Ways To Reverence God More

It's popular these days to say about TV shows and more, 'It's totally irreverent!" People usually mean it's hot and you should enjoy it. But before you start saying that as a hot thing to say. Here's a couple of people in the Bible who were considered irreverent.

Cain was warned about the sin crouching at his door. Yet, he disregarded it when he brought God the common sacrifice and offering instead of the first and the best like his brother Abel.

As you know, he got so jealous of Abel's favor and blessing because of his obedient offering, he killed his brother and became the first murderer. By faith, Abel still speaks today. His obedience tells us to be reverent of our God and his way.

Esau was irreverent and disrespectful of the things of God. The Bible described Esau as, despising the things of God. In Genesis 25:34, "Then Jacob gave Esau some bread and lentil stew. Esau ate the meal, then got up and left. He showed contempt for his rights as the firstborn."

And then again the Hebrew writer warns us about taking on the attitude and actions of Esau, "See that no one is sexually immoral, or is godless like Esau, who for a single meal sold his inheritance rights as the oldest son. Afterward, as you know, when he wanted to inherit this blessing, he was rejected. Even though he sought the blessing with tears, he could not change what he had done." —Hebrews 12:16,17

As Christians, we have to guard against the ways of the world. The word of God says, we should work hard to stay unpolluted from the world. The writer of James says, "Pure and genuine religion in the sight of God the Father means caring for orphans and widows in their distress and refusing to let the world corrupt you." —James 1:27

So, to be reverent, respectful (fear) of God is how we should want to be. To do that, let's look at what reverence means generally, 'deep respect for someone or something. regard or treat with deep respect.

'When Jesus taught the disciples to pray, he started with Our Father, Who are in heaven, holy is your name..." He essentially taught them and now us, to reverence our heavenly Father daily.

I encourage you to make reverence a part of your worship time. Even in Jesus' prayer pattern, he starts by reverencing the name of God. With all of that said, here are some good reasons to reverence our God in our irreverent world and society. When we reverence (fear, respect) God, we can expect to:

1. Receive the key to salvation, wisdom and knowledge.

He will be the sure foundation for your times, a rich store of salvation and wisdom and knowledge; reverence of the LORD is the key to this treasure. -Isaiah 33:6

2. Help us live a clean life.

By lovingkindness and truth iniquity is atoned for, And by reverence of the LORD one keeps away from evil. -Proverbs 16:6

3. Show that we are children of the light.

Always giving thanks for all things in the name of our Lord Jesus Christ to God, even the Father; and be subject to one another in reverence of Christ. -Ephesians 5:21

4. Live in a secure fortress.

Whoever reverences the LORD has a secure fortress, and for their children it will be a refuge. - Proverbs 14:26

5. Give A fountain of life.

Reverence of the LORD is a life-giving fountain; it offers escape from the snares of death. -Proverbs 14:27

6. Cultivate Gratefulness.

Only reverence the LORD and serve Him in truth with all your heart; for consider what great things He has done for you. -1 Samuel 12:24

7. Build us up in the church.

So the church throughout all Judea and Galilee and Samaria enjoyed peace, being built up; and going on in reverence of the Lord and in the comfort of the Holy Spirit, it continued to increase. –Acts 9:31

8. Bring security and protection.

Reverence of the LORD leads to life, bringing security and protection from harm. –Proverbs 19:23

9. Enjoy a longer life.

Reverence of the LORD adds length to life, but the years of the wicked are cut short. –Proverbs 10:27

17. Know your destiny.

Who are those who reverence the LORD? He will show them the path they should choose. –Psalm 25:12

So, won't you join me in learning to reverence, respect and fear our God more and more. I pray your faith is encouraged to live a respectful, reverent life before Him, guarding against being polluted by the world as night approaches.

As you reverence God more and more, he will direct your path and make sure you have a legacy worth leaving. Remember, any legacy you leave is not by your might or even your authority but by the Spirit of the Lord.

Legacy Snippet

Victory Is On The Way!

Twenty-one years ago, I joined a new-to-us church called Covenant Church. My husband and I had been married two years at that time. So, CC was not the only thing new in my life. Before CC and before my new husband, I was pretty beat up by life and an abusive marriage.

Inside, I was still broken and walking like a monkey with my hands to the ground. How do I know? God mercifully showed me the state of my inner man.

I say mercifully because as it is with any struggle and victory, you have to know there is a problem, acknowledge the problem and do what it takes to fix it, right? It's that way with alcoholism, drug addiction, weight loss, a wounded spirit and I suspect most things in life that we're challenged with.

With God All Things Are Possible!

My conversation with Father God went something like this: O.k., Father I know this is not good that I'm walking around like this. I know it was you that delivered me from those circumstances as a victim of spouse abuse. And not only that, after being single for five years you gave me a caring and beautiful husband in Varn.

My outer physical wounds are healed. But how do I fix the inside? It's not like me or anyone else can reach in straighten me upright and lift my head. Immediately, the words came to me, "With man it's impossible but with God all things are possible."

Now, this is a part of my testimony; so I get to present (as a friend of mine calls it) my grace trophy, a lot. I noticed something, not long ago, about these words. The Holy Spirit is honest. He acknowledged to me that it was an impossible thing but with God all things become possible.

With those words, I began a journey to victory. God became the lifter of my head and gave me a beautiful testimony of healing and the restoration of my soul. —Psalm 3:3 I put those steps to victory of my soul in the first WOW Women book called WOW Women of Worth located at http://wowontheweb.com. Here's how it all started for me.

Shortly after joining my church, I had an epiphany1 while listening to my pastor preach. It was around the Easter and Mother's Day season.

He broke the message of Christ down to understandable terms. He presented Christ the Lamb of God. He once again explained the message of Christ, our substitute and the terrible price that was paid for our redemption which included salvation, healing, prosperity, our victory, our everything. He explained the transaction of heaven that reconciled humanity to their creator and Father God. It created redemption for the whole world and the opportunity for them to receive it.

Then with all somberness and clarity he asked the congregation, "Why haven't you received your victory yet? He went on to say, I know this could sound a bit harsh. But what I'm saying is Christ died on the cross for you. He paid a horrible price. What more can He do? His work is FINISHED.

That's where the 'finished work of Christ' phrase comes from. This is what our Lord was talking about when on the cross, he said, "It is finished!" The Bible tells us His price was sufficient, even more than enough. Now it's up to YOU to receive. In fact, you shun the sacrifice of Christ by not activating your faith."

My Epiphany

He went on to say, "It comes down to why are you not taking advantage of all that's been prepared for you. This whole church and everything in it is designed to train you, even equip you for a victorious life in Christ.

I mean every Sunday, Wednesday Night and/or Saturday service program, Bible class and small group are ALL designed to help YOU gain that victory. All you have to do is:

Sign up and show up. Take the first step, submit yourself to God and keep walking with believers to your finish line, YOUR VICTORY..."

My epiphany was after hearing that message, I had no excuse for not receiving victory in every area of my life that I needed. And my friend, most importantly now, neither do you...

That next morning, I sat before God and said I'm not moving from this spot in prayer until I hear from heaven. If it takes days, weeks, months every time I pray I will come right back to this spot. I have to know what I must say or do to receive my victory.

Then I said Lord whatever you instruct me to do I'll do it. If you want me to sign up, sit down, do more, wait on you, whatever it is, I'll do it.

You know the ending to this story already. When I got serious and tenacious, God got serious with me. It turned out He answered that day. I began my journey to victory that very day. It was not instantaneous but it was sure. It was a process that I had to trust God through but I received my victory.

Victory is on the way for you!

Now I turn to you and ask, "Why haven't you received your deliverance? Why haven't you walked in your destiny? Why haven't you started on your journey? Why haven't you pursued God to victory?" God sent His Son Jesus as your substitute. Jesus paid a horrible price so YOU could have life and life more abundantly.

Every Apostle, Prophet, Pastor, Teacher, Elder and Leader of God have been commissioned to equip you for maturity and victory in Christ. Every part of the Body of Christ inside the local church was designed to lift you to victory. If you don't find any such life-giving sources in your church, go where you know the Spirit of God has liberty.

Remember, Christ is our propitiation, the sacrificial Lamb of God. He started and still builds His modern-day church for you.

...for all have sinned and fall short of the glory of God, being justified freely by His grace through the redemption that is in Christ Jesus, whom God set forth as a propitiation by His blood through faith, to demonstrate His righteousness, because in His Forbearance God had passed over the sins that were previously committed.

After Jesus left this earth rising into the sky and clouds while his early church disciples watched, days later He did what he promised to do. He sent the gift of the Holy Spirit to comfort us, to guide and help us as the paracletos, the Counselor.

If not already, receive the gift of the Holy Spirit. "But when the Counselor comes, whom I shall send to you from the Father, even the Spirit of truth, who proceeds from the Father, he will bear witness to Me." —John 15:26

Benefits Not Automatic

Even so, Jesus paid the price and there are beautiful benefits that are available to us in His substitutionary work. None of the blessing or inheritance of God work automatically, even though they belong to us. They become manifested in our lives or we experience the victory paid for by Christ as we exercise our faith to receive them.

Each work must be appropriated and received by faith. Our salvation, healing, deliverance, our prosperity and everything else must be received by faith. A choice or a decision of faith must be made. You can choose today to receive your breakthrough by faith. The victory could be yours NOW through faith.

On Calvary and through His resurrection Christ fulfilled the words of the Prophet Isaiah,

"Surely He has borne our grief and carried our sorrows; yet we esteemed Him stricken smitten by God and afflicted. But He was wounded for our transgressions. He was bruised for our iniquities. The chastisement for our peace was upon Him and by His stripes, we are healed." Isaiah 53:4.5

It's in the receiving now. My prayer is that if you're anything like I was years ago, you know, fed up with being fed up and ready for a breakthrough now. Through the finished work of Christ, and His church, you can have it. You can stop counting Christ's sacrifice lightly.

You can start honoring Him today, right now even, by receiving by faith what He paid such a horrible price for. The Holy Spirit of God is ready to walk you through. You can receive by faith your victory, your healing, your deliverance, even your breakthrough. I received mine; why not you?

Summing It All Up

Ready to defeat the giants of your generation? Two women faced with a hard decision at the crossroads of life. Either way, their destinies would be changed. One chose to go back and the other chose to go forward. They both grew to become historic matriarchs in the lives of their family and the people of God.

Through God's sovereignty the results resound through the centuries to now. What did they use to change their destiny, their future and the lives of others forever? They used the secret power of choice to pivot their destiny and leave a legacy, like no other.

I realized afresh giants can be scary, real or perceived. So, I'm glad we have a God that loves us. He has sent angels to minister to and help us. We can know, he fights for us; the battle is not ours but his. So, any giant screaming obscenities to your generation is a defeated foe.

Somberly, I realized it doesn't mean it's not dangerous. Most battles are dangerous. For we must fight God's way; get his instructions and depend on him to defeat the giants of our generations.

Furthermore, we thank God that all Scripture is God-breathed and inspired by him. It is useful for instruction and setting a great pattern that we can follow.

Through the choice of hope Ruth made and the heart of repentance and obedience of her great-grandson King David, we are inspired to overcome the giants in our generation.

We can take up the five smooth stones of revelation and throw the Rock of Ages and hit our giant enemy right between the eyes. Run up with the sword of the Spirit and chop his head off. Then shout for the victory is ours, even to our children's children! Hallelujah!

Legacy Challenge 4

Write down the three scriptures that stood out to you the most, from the '11 Ways To Reverence God More and More section. Meditate on them this week or as long you want. Write down what God speaks to you about them.

Chapter Five

Passing the torch Of Legacy

A Woman's Passing Of The Torch

I am reminded of your sincere faith, which first lived in your grandmother Lois and in your mother Eunice and, I am persuaded, now lives in you also. 2 Timothy 1:5

Lois and Eunice are commended for their personal faith in the New Testament. With God's help, they rose above the rest, in their personal faith and preparing their life as a pattern to pass. What did they do that caught the attention of the Apostle Paul and passed their faith forward to the third generation?

These two women became famous for raising a godly young man in the midst of an ungodly society. They prepared a torch of legacy for the generations to come. He was the Apostle Paul's most trusted companion, disciple and beloved son of the gospel.

It Acts 1:6 and 2 Timothy 1:5 we discover these women with a strong commendation from the Apostle Paul. He writes: "I have been reminded of your sincere faith, which first lived in your grandmother Lois and in your mother Eunice and, I am persuaded, now lives in you also." These women were credited with passing their faith on to the next generation.

Beginning A Legacy

5 Glorious Reasons To Walk In His Will And His Way

So don't worry about tomorrow, for tomorrow will bring its own worries. Today's trouble is enough for today. Matthew 6:33,34l

Lois and Eunice became famous for their unfeigned faith, walking in God's will and his way. They passed that same faith to their Timotheus.

But before Paul and Timothy, a disciple came to Jesus asking, "Lord teach us to pray," also, with unfeigned faith. Jesus immediately gave them and now us a pattern, even a model prayer to pray.

He directed us to reverence Father God first of all, then to ask for God's way and his will to be done in our lives.

Remember, "Our Father who are heaven, holy is your name; your kingdom come (way of doings things; government), your will be done (word of God) on earth as it is in heaven...

Which brings me to the principle, we're discussing today, Father God has a way of doing things that he wants us to follow.

Essentially, his way is the kingdom of God. In fact, he commands us to 'seek first the kingdom of God and all other things will be added unto us.'

Just for clarification, kingdom is domain, rulership, way of doing things. When you are born again as a Christian, you are under another kingdom.

You are translated, born again, saved into this kingdom of God, a kingdom of light. In the kingdom of God, there is no lack. There is no curse. There is plenty of provision, already.

The curse was eradicated by the death, burial and resurrection of Jesus Christ. There is peace and prosperity. Father God has ALREADY made you more wealthy than your wildest dreams. The blessing was made ready to activate by faith in God's covenant with believers in Jesus.

Sacrificial and redemptive, the blood of Jesus was applied to the mercy seat of God, once and for all. Doing it Father God's way, Jesus suffered, died on the cross, was buried and rose again. After the finished work, he has sat down at the right hand of the Father to wait for his enemies to become his foot stool. Here are five glorious reasons to walk in His will and His way:

1. Live His way and have a happy life.

"So don't worry about tomorrow, for tomorrow will bring its own worries. Today's trouble is enough for today. Matthew 6:33,34

2. Pray his way and get answers to prayer.

These things I have written to you who believe in the name of the Son of God, so that you may know that you have eternal life. This is the confidence which we have before Him, that, if we ask anything according to His will, He hears us. And if we know that He hears us in whatever we ask, we know that we have the requests which we have asked from Him.... -1 John 5:13,14,15

3. Think His thoughts, learn his ways and fulfill his plans.

"For My thoughts are not your thoughts, Nor are your ways My ways," declares the LORD. "For as the heavens are higher than the earth, So are My ways higher than your ways And My thoughts than your thoughts. "For as the rain and the snow come down from heaven, And do not return there without watering the earth
And making it bear and sprout, And furnishing seed to the sower and bread to the eater; So will My word be which goes forth from My mouth; It will not return to Me empty, Without accomplishing what I desire, And without succeeding in the matter for which I sent it....... -Isaiah 55:8-11

4. Know his way is to trouble those who trouble you.

God is just: He will pay back trouble to those who trouble you. 1 Thessalonians 4:6

5. Commit your way to the Lord and trust him to receive his way, his plan, your destiny.

Delight yourself in the LORD; And He will give you the desires of your heart. Commit your way to the LORD, Trust also in Him, and He will do it. He will bring forth your righteousness as the light And your judgment as the noonday....-Psalm 37:5

Now, keep going in God's way and his will. Begin to deposit God's word into your heart and watch your life blossom into God's ways.

Building Your Legacy

The Hope Of Heaven

Because of the hope laid up for you in heaven, of which you previously heard in the word of truth, the gospel. -Colossians 1:5

Hopefully, you've been enjoying this chapter, 'Passing The Torch Of Legacy'. Our hope for heaven is the ultimate blessing and legacy that God has designed for his people. Jesus has gone ahead of us and prepared a place for us. We've discovered more and more; our Lord plans us to live a blessed life as well.

So, where are you headed, heaven or hell? It's a good question. Because whether you believe in either place, one day the decision will be evident. For man is appointed once to die then the judgment. —Hebrews 9:27

We live only once, then if Jesus tarries, we all leave the land of the living, by way of death.

Wait! Before you tune me out for the doom and gloom, there's good news! This really is a good news message. It's the story of God's recompense. You see, God so loved the world that he gave his only begotten son, Jesus. He essentially purchased the world back, therefore he redeemed the world through the sacrificial death of His son.

But let me back up a little, to tell the story of God's Recompense.

It began in the Garden of Eden. In the beginning, with Adam and Eve. They were blessed and commanded to multiply, replenish and given authority over the earth. Adam and Eve sinned and unwittingly gave their authority away. Eve was deceived by the Serpent and Adam who knew better gave in to Eve's invitation to eat from the tree they had been commanded not to eat from.

After their mistakes, there was a fallen earth (world). judgment was rendered to all parties involved. As you may know, they each received a portion of the curse. Through the sin of the first couple, the authority over the earth was relinquished to the Serpent, now called Satan.

Our ability to receive the blessing, multiply and replenish was hindered.

The good news is Father God had a plan to redeem the world. Yet, I did say HAD. His redemption plan, also began in the Garden of Eden when he prophesied, "And I will put enmity between thee and the woman, and between thy seed and her seed; it shall bruise thy head, and thou shalt bruise his heel."

Therefore, we have in Genesis 3:15, the first promise of a Redeemer. It became a long line of prophecies concerning the coming Savior and Redeemer of the world. The Seed, the Promised One would be from the woman's seed a sign of the eventual virgin birth of Christ.

His ultimate plan stretched down through the ages, slipped under the radar of the enemy, who inspired the Romans and the Jews of that day to crucify Jesus on the cross, unwittingly killing, and sacrificing the innocent lamb.

The one that had been prophesied and foretold since the beginning of time. In the fullness of time, through God's foreordained plan the Redeemer was born.

Let me be clear, the simple truth, there is only one way to get to heaven. That one way is believing in the Lord Jesus Christ. If you confess with your mouth Jesus as Lord, and believe in your heart that God raised Him from the dead, you will be saved; for with the heart a person believes, resulting in righteousness, and with the mouth he confesses, resulting in salvation. — Romans 10:10

On with the story, because of the Fall, every human being is by nature a sinful being. The Bible says that our efforts at doing 'good deeds' are not acceptable in the sight of God. For by grace you have been saved through faith. And this is not your own doing; it is the gift of God, not a result of works, so that no one may boast. — Ephesians 2:8-9

So we can say, God alone is holy. He alone is good. Yet, God has made a way for sinful human beings to enter into heaven. Although, he alone is holy. He commands us to be holy as well. How can we, sinful humans that we are be holy and righteous before a holy God?

A Call to Be Holy

...but like the Holy One who called you, be holy yourselves also in all your behavior; because it is written, "YOU SHALL BE HOLY, FOR I AM HOLY." If you address as Father the One who impartially judges according to each one's work, conduct yourselves in fear during the time of your stay on earth -1 Peter 1:16,17

Let's continue, the answer to that question can be found in God's story of recompense. As we discussed earlier, Father God had a redemption plan back in the Garden of Eden, when Adam and Eve first sinned. Over 2000 years ago, this plan came to fruition. He sent his son, Jesus as the redeemer. Remember, for God so loved the world that he gave his only begotten son.

His mother Mary was a virgin. She was impregnated by the Holy Spirit of the Living God. She gave birth to the Son of God, the Lord Jesus Christ.

God's law required that a life be taken to save a life. In essence that blood be shed to ratify a covenant. For a time, an appointed Jewish priest offered animal sacrifices annually to cover the chosen people's sin.

But God had a better and permanent solution that would settle it once and for ALL. It doesn't have to be renewed and redone year after year.

In that way, the New Covenant is a better covenant. As it was revealed that ALL included the whole world. So, God sacrificed His only son, through the Person of the Lord Jesus Christ, so that our sins could be forgiven and cleansed through his blood.

During His time on earth, Jesus led a perfect, sinless life and the ultimate price for the sin of the world. Now, let's take a look at what the Bible says about our hope of heaven.

What The Bible Says About The Hope of Heaven

Heaven IS and WILL BE:

•An Inheritance For The Children Of God:

"Praise be to the God and Father of our Lord Jesus Christ! In his great mercy he has given us new birth into a living hope through the resurrection of Jesus Christ from the dead, and into an inheritance that can never perish, spoil or fade. This inheritance is kept in heaven for you" (1 Peter 1:3-4).

"Then the sovereignty, power and greatness of all the kingdoms under heaven will be handed over to the holy people of the Most High. His kingdom will be an everlasting kingdom, and all rulers will worship and obey him" (Daniel 7:27).

•A Heavenly Home for Each Believer:

Jesus said to His disciples, "Do not let your hearts be troubled. You believe in God; believe also in me. My Father's house has many rooms; if that were not so, would I have told you that I am going there to prepare a place for you? And if I go and prepare a place for you, I will come back and take you to be with me that you also may be where I am" (John 14:1-3).

The Apostle Paul wrote "...our citizenship is in heaven. And we eagerly await a Savior from there, the Lord Jesus Christ" (Philippians 3:20).

•A Place Believers Can Live Forever:

Jesus said, "Everyone who has heard the Father and learned from him comes to me. ... Very truly I tell you, the one who believes has eternal life. I am the bread of life. ... I am the living bread that came down from heaven. Whoever eats this bread will live forever" (John 6:45, 47, 48, 51).

"To the one who is victorious, I will give the right to eat from the tree of life, which is in the paradise of God "(Revelation 2:11).

Jesus Christ died on the cross at Skull Hill, Golgotha. He was buried in the tomb, Joseph Arimathea for three days and, on the third day, He was raised from the dead. After forty days, He returned to heaven, where He currently reigns, sitting at the right hand of the Father.

And He will return to earth a second time to claim those who have confessed their belief in Him. Make we be ready, for the Hope of Heaven. For surely, Jesus will return again!

Strengthening Your Legacy

More Hope Of Heaven

How to get to heaven - Make it so

Know that Jesus died so those who believe in Him would no longer be condemned to an eternity apart from God.

If you want to seal the hope of going to heaven after you die and you believe that Jesus Christ died to save you from the judgement and penalty for your sins, answer these questions.

Am I a sinner, even though I live a pretty good life? I've never even let alcohol touch my lips. I haven't murdered anyone.

First of all, we are all sinners, no matter how good or evil we think we are. No man can boast of his goodness. We inherited a sinful nature just by being born. With that said, do you understand that you are a sinner?

Do you believe that Jesus Christ came as the one and only Redeemer of sin? Are you ready to receive God's gift of His Son, Jesus Christ? If so, believe in Christ, repent of your sins, and commit the rest of your life to Him as Lord. Pray like this:

1. **Father, I know that I have sinned** and my sins have separated me from you. I am sorry, and now I want to turn away from my past sinful life toward you. Please forgive me, and help me stop sinning. I believe that your son, Jesus Christ died for my sins. I believe he was buried, resurrected from the dead, now is alive and hears my prayer.

2. **I invite Jesus to become the Lord of my life,** to rule and reign in my heart from <<<<this day forward>>> _____. Please fill me with your Holy Spirit to help me obey You, and to do Your will for the rest of my life. In Jesus' name I pray, Amen." "Repent, and let every one of you be baptized in the name of Jesus Christ for the remission of sins; and you shall receive the gift of the Holy Spirit" (Acts 2:38). Jesus Christ died on the cross at Skull Hill, Golgatha. He was buried in the tomb, Joseph Arithea for three days and, on the third day, He was raised from the dead. After forty days, He returned to heaven, where He currently reigns, sitting at the right hand of the Father.

And He will return to earth a second time to claim those who have confessed their belief in Him.

If you received Jesus today, welcome to God's family. Now, as a way to grow closer to Him, the Bible tells us to seal our commitment. Here are five ways to seal your commitment. Do this and it will be life changing and life-long.

1. Get baptized as commanded by Christ.
2. Tell someone else about your new faith in Christ.
3. Spend time with God each day. It does not have to be a long period of time. Just develop the daily habit of praying to Him and reading His Word. Ask God to increase your faith and your understanding of the Bible.
4. Seek fellowship with other followers of Jesus. Develop a group of believing friends to answer your questions and support you.
5. Find a local church where you can worship God.

Six More Things The Bible Says About The Hope Of Heaven

• A Place of Worship to God:

"Then I looked and heard the voice of many angels, numbering thousands upon thousands, and ten thousand times ten thousand. They encircled the throne and the living creatures and the elders. In a loud voice they were saying: 'Worthy is the Lamb, who was slain, to receive power and wealth and wisdom and strength and honor and glory and praise!' Then I heard every creature in heaven and on earth and under the earth and on the sea, and all that is in them, saying: 'To him who sits on the throne and to the Lamb be praise and honor and glory and power, for ever and ever!' The four living creatures said, 'Amen,' and the elders fell down and worshiped" — Revelation 5:11-14.

• Where We Are Entirely Righteous:

"You ought to live holy and godly lives as you look forward to the day of God and speed its coming. That day will bring about the destruction of the heavens by fire, and the elements will melt in the heat. But in keeping with his promise we are looking forward to a new heaven and a new earth, where righteousness dwells" —2 Peter 3:11-13.

• Where Things Are New:

God said to the prophet Isaiah, "See, I will create new heavens and a new earth. The former things will not be remembered, nor will they come to mind" —Isaiah 65:17.

• A Place Where Peace And Joy Reigns:

"…They will beat their swords into plowshares and their spears into pruning hooks. Nation will not take up sword against nation, nor will they train for war anymore. … You will go out in joy and be led forth in peace; the mountains and hills will burst into song before you, and all the trees of the field will clap their hands" —Isaiah 2:4; Isaiah 55:12.

• A Place For The Humble Not Just The Rich And Famous:

"Jesus told His disciples, '… unless you change and become like little children, you will never enter the kingdom of heaven. Therefore, whoever takes the lowly position of this child is the greatest in the kingdom of heaven. … Truly I tell you, it is hard for someone who is rich to enter the kingdom of heaven'" —Matthew 18:3-5; Matthew 19:23.

• A Place Of Unity:

"While they were eating, Jesus took bread, and when he had given thanks, he broke it and gave it to his disciples, saying, 'Take it; this is my body.' Then he took a cup, and when he had given thanks, he gave it to them, and they all drank from it.

'This is my blood of the covenant, which is poured out for many,' he said to them. 'Truly I tell you, I will not drink again from the fruit of the vine until that day when I drink it new in the kingdom of God'" —Mark 14:22-25.

A Legacy Of Grace

10 More Ways To Walk In His Glorious Will And His Way

Over the years, immature and sometimes disobedient, I've sought to go my own way. I can testify my way has never worked well for me. And neither will yours.

I've finally said, it was good that I was afflicted, that I might greatly desire God's will and his way.

Those words came out of my spirit man. They are reminiscent of another person who had revelation on this matter. He said, 'It was good that I was afflicted so that I might not go astray...'

Or the Apostle Paul who after many trials and tribulations, "Concerning this I implored the Lord three times that it might leave me. And He has said to me,

"My grace is sufficient for you, for power is perfected in weakness." Most gladly, therefore, I will rather boast about my weaknesses, so that the power of Christ may dwell in me.

Therefore, I am well content with weaknesses, with insults, with distresses, with persecutions, with difficulties, for Christ's sake; for when I am weak, then I am strong... -2 Corinthians 12:9

Finally, our Lord Jesus, and greatest example, he learned obedience through suffering, just as we must do also.

During the days of Jesus' life on earth, he offered up prayers and petitions with fervent cries and tears to the one who could save him from death, and he was heard because of his reverent submission. Even though Jesus was God's Son, he learned obedience from the things he suffered.

In this way, God qualified him as a perfect High Priest, and he became the source of eternal salvation for all those who obey him. -Hebrews 5:7,8,9

In the Garden of Gethsemane, we find Jesus, kneeling alone praying with such intensity that has sweat rolling off his face as great drops of blood. 'If it be your will, let this cup pass from me.

Nevertheless, your will be done..." And so it was, God's will and His way. Just as he warned earlier the disciples, he was handed over and suffered greatly at their hands.

It was God's way, through his son Jesus that the earth and humanity be reclaimed from the hands of Satan.

With all that said, don't be afraid. He has promised never to leave you or forsake you. Our God is a loving father. He works all things to our good. He never wastes our pain and promises to pay back for every trouble and tribulation on this side of heaven or the next. He always recompenses. Here are some more glorious tips to make sure you are walking in God's way and his will:

1. Seek God's way and everything else will be added to you.

Seek the Kingdom of God above all else, and live righteously, and he will give you everything you need Matthew 6:33

2. Know God's word and be confident in him.

This is the confidence we have in approaching God: that if we ask anything according to his will, he hears us. And if we know he hears us then we know we have what we've asked of him. -1 John 5:14,15

3. Don't depend on your own understanding but trust God

Trust in the LORD with all your heart; do not depend on your own understanding. -Proverbs 3:5

4. Commit your way to the Lord

Commit everything you do to the LORD. Trust him, and he will help you. -Psalm 37:5

5. Commit whatever you do to the Lord and your plans will be successful.

Commit your activities to the LORD, and your plans will succeed. -Psalm 16:3

6. Learn little by little

He tells us everything over and over--one line at a time, one line at a time, a little here, and a little there!" Isaiah 28:10

7. Attend a local church.

And let us not neglect our meeting together, as some people do, but encourage one another, especially now that the day of his return is drawing near. -Hebrews 10:25

8. Understand that humility comes before honor.

Fear of the LORD teaches wisdom; humility precedes honor. Proverbs 15:33

9. Reverence him and he shows us our destiny.

Who are those who reverence the LORD? He will show them the path they should choose. Psalm 25:12

10. Proclaim God to the next generation.

Let me proclaim your power to this new generation, your mighty miracles to all who come after me. -Psalm 71:18

Renew your mind, watch yourself transform into a new creature for Christ. Just as Prophet Isaiah proclaimed, his thoughts and his ways are higher than ours but it doesn't have to be that way. Because of God's guarantee, he will watch over his word in our lives to perform it.

Legacy Snippet

A Woman's Baton Of Legacy

Tell your children about it in the years to come, and let your children tell their children. Pass the story down from generation to generation. —Joel 1:3

Have you seen a race where they pass the baton, one to another, recently? It truly amazes me to see how our little child hood games can speak to us in life, if we allow it to. In this race of passing the baton, the main objective is the team with the baton to cross the finish line with the help of each other.

The one who crosses the finish line first with the baton wins. Another thing to realize, is the greatest opportunity for mishap is during the pass. It takes skill, focus and determination to successfully pass to the receiver.

Now what does that symbolize spiritually to you and me. The word of God tells us to run the race with all diligence, being prepared in all diligence. What's symbolic of it, is a race that's not run by ourselves, it includes others, so not only our generation but the ones to come.

Are You In Preparation To Pass The Baton?

We serve a God that's generational in thinking. Remember, Abraham, Isaac and Jacob. You know that it's good to be a success but it is really noted to train a good successor when you are leaving provision for the next generation, and the ones after that. We must make sure that we are in the right mold of thinking. We should not just have a "Me, Myself and I" kind of thinking.

Here's what King Hezekiah did about the matter:

Hezekiah became king when he was twenty-five years old; and he reigned twenty-nine years in Jerusalem. And his mother's name was Abijah, the daughter of Zechariah. He did right in the sight of the LORD, according to all that his father David had done.

In the first year of his reign, in the first month, he opened the doors of the house of the LORD and repaired them. He brought in the priests and the Levites and gathered them into the square on the east.

Reform Begun

Then he said to them, "Listen to me, O Levites. Consecrate yourselves now, and consecrate the house of the LORD, the God of your fathers, and carry the uncleanness out from the holy place. "For our fathers have been unfaithful and have done evil in the sight of the LORD our God, and have forsaken Him and turned their faces away from the dwelling place of the LORD, and have turned their backs.

"They have also shut the doors of the porch and put out the lamps, and have not burned incense or offered burnt offerings in the holy place to the God of Israel.

"Therefore the wrath of the LORD was against Judah and Jerusalem, and He has made them an object of terror, of horror, and of hissing, as you see with your own eyes. "For behold, our fathers have fallen by the sword, and our sons and our daughters and our wives are in captivity for this.

"Now it is in my heart to make a covenant with the LORD God of Israel, that His burning anger may turn away from us.

"My sons, do not be negligent now, for the LORD has chosen you to stand before Him, to minister to Him, and to be His ministers and burn incense." II Chronicles 29:1-11

The Challenge In Passing The Baton

As a leader you must be willing to delegate your authority and give what the Lord has given to you, to your successor. A good leader will always be reproducing themselves within their team.

Because, as a faithful servant, the Lord may be preparing to promote you to a higher position/another level. And how can he do it, if you have no one prepared to take your place?

We serve a God of order and completion. If we are following his way, we are continually going from level to level and glory to glory. He wants us to follow his pattern of producing good leadership for the kingdom of God.

Done this way, the pattern can go that step further of generation to generation. Won't you join us in preparing a baton to pass to our successors and even the next generation.

Summing It All Up

Are you preparing a baton to pass to the next generation yet? I get a happy thought whenever I think about the fact that we serve a God that's generational in thinking. Throughout the Bible, he mentions several generations in passing information and most importantly making covenant.

It's the same way with you and me. The promises of God are for us and our children. A person can be a noted successful person to build a dynasty, an empire in their lifetime. We discovered it becomes really extraordinary when you find a person that has generational vision.

It was encouraging to study Lois and Eunice who were commended for their personal faith in the New Testament. With God's help, they rose above the rest, in their personal faith and preparing their life as a legacy to pass.

Catching the Apostle's attention, they became famous for raising the godly young man, Timothy in the midst of an ungodly society. They prepared a torch of legacy for the generations to come. He turned out to be the Apostle Paul's most trusted companion, disciple and beloved son of the gospel.

Now, it's our turn. Who are you mentoring and pouring into? If not already, get started praying about someone today. Start living your life as a legacy.

Legacy Challenge 5

It's God's way that we learn a little by little. He knows we are frail creatures. So, as not to overwhelm us, He gives his instructions, his leading to us step by step. He tells us everything over and over--one line at a time, one line at a time, a little here, and a little there!" —Isaiah 28:10 Write below your favorite scripture from the God's Way and His Will section. Meditate on it this week or as long as you want.

Chapter Six

Living A Life Of Legacy

A Woman's Life Well Lived

And Mary said, Behold the handmaid of the Lord; be it unto me according to thy word. And the angel departed from her. —Luke 1:38

er humility brought her before the angel sent with a holy message from God. Her response to the angel caused her to receive a 400-year-old prophecy fulfilled. Mary, a virgin gave birth to a child and called his name, Jesus. God's glorious plan of salvation for mankind was consummated through Jesus.

What did Mary know that brought her from giving birth to Jesus in a stable to being numbered in the Upper Room on the Day of Pentecost? She used the secret power of a 'yielded vessel' to multiply her future and the destiny of countless.

Mary became the epitome of a faithful mother. A virgin, she yielded to the Spirit of God and became pregnant with the Son of God, thereby fulfilling Scripture. She responded in faith to the angel Gabriel. She lived her life in faith as the mother of Jesus. She watched in faith as he died a humiliating death on the cross, paying the ultimate price for our sins. She was in the Upper Room waiting on the Comforter to come, sent by Jesus, as he promised. She lived a legacy that moved the world.

Beginning A Legacy

The Blessed Life

It's in Christ that we find out who we are and what we are living for. Long before we first heard of Christ and got our hopes up, he had his eye on us, had design on us for glorious living, with part of the overall purpose he is working out in everything and everyone. — Ephesians 1:11,12

My spiritual gifting didn't seem like a gift at first. In fact, it felt more like a curse. And I surely didn't think it was something to be passed on. I counseled several times on different occasions with my church leaders. I tried to find someone that would explain these happenings to me.

I found no one that even came close to what I thought I needed. The Holy Spirit finally got across to me that he was going to teach me himself. For years, I now know Father God has trained me and still is training me by his Spirit. Which brings me to my point in this last chapter.

You may have noticed by now; I don't have a one-two-three-point plan to offer about building legacy. I believe it's because by his Spirit God wants to teach you himself. He wants to take you by the hand and lead you in the way you should go. He wants to write his word upon your heart just like the Bible says he will do.

This is what the Prophet Jeremiah prophesied about the New Covenant, "But this is the covenant which I will make with the house of Israel after those days," declares the LORD, "I will put My law within them and on their heart I will write it; and I will be their God, and they shall be My people... Jeremiah 31:32-34

The truth is we live our life the best we can in God and he gives us posterity. My best advice is to become a 'yielded vessel' like our featured WOW! Woman, Mary the mother of Jesus. Her simplicity of faith and grace reaches through the generations or like our father in the faith, Abraham. God gave him a posterity like the stars of the heaven.

Getting Saved Is Progressive

Remember, being saved is progressive. We are continuously being saved in some area of our life. That's why the New Testament writer says, we work out our salvation with fear and trembling. As God wills, we appropriate his mercy. Line by line, precept by precept, we are transformed...

The Greek word and verb 'Sozo' meaning to 'to save' includes every part of man's being. The Apostle Paul eloquently sums it up with 1 Thessalonians 5:23 "Now may the God of peace Himself sanctify you completely; and may your whole spirit, soul and body be presented blameless at the coming of our Lord Jesus Christ."

Therefore, we can say salvation includes the total human personality -- spirit, soul and body and it is consummated only by the resurrection of the body, at the return of Jesus Christ.

Living the Blessing - God's Will And His Way

I talked about this earlier. So, again I say God is sovereign, meaning he's in charge. So, I can say, it's by faith and revelation that we receive this abundant provisions of mercy, the blessing. God, sovereignly, ordains and orders that we receive each provision. He discerns the motives and even the state of our heart. So, when we approach the throne boldly on the basis of Christ's sacrifice, we still need to be sensitive to the leading of the Holy Spirit.

Allow Father God to save in the order, he chooses and sees fit. For example, most of us want to receive prosperity first but God may want us to focus on receiving His righteous, his sanctification and then his prosperity. Or he may want to heal us before we can receive forgiveness. If we stubbornly claim and ask for we want or think is right we may not receive either.

Confessing The Blessing

The Greek word Paul uses here to describe God's word is Rhema. This is primarily a word that is spoken. It becomes effective only when it is spoken through believing lips. The Ephesian writer encourages us to take up the sword of the Spirit, which is the Word of God. Ephesians 6:17 You can be sure there is no middle ground.

According to Derek Prince in his 1990 book Blessing or Curse, "We either do one of three things: make a positive, scriptural confession; make no confession or make a negative unscriptural confession.

Jesus proclaimed the word of God. The Apostles proclaimed the word of God and so should we. Proclamation 'Latin verb' shout forth or shout aloud suggest strong, confident assertion of faith, thanksgiving and praise. We thank God for what He does; We praise Him for Who He is.

First we raise the banner of proclamation. We speak out boldly, in faith, the promise or the provision of God's word that applies to our particular situation or meets our particular need. Then we go on to thank God -- still in faith - for the truth we have proclaimed.

Finally, we move from thanksgiving to jubilant praise. All this we do in pure faith without waiting for any visible change in our situation. Enter into His gates with thanksgiving and into Hi courts with praise. Be thankful to Him and bless His name. −Psalm 100:4" Start now, confessing the word of God through praying, speaking and proclaiming. Here are three confessions to get started:

1.   Enter into the blessings of Abraham

Through the sacrifice of Jesus on the cross. I have passed out from under the curse and entered into the blessings of Abraham, whom God blessed in all things. based on Galatians 3:13-14

2.   Hold onto your confessions of hope

And having a High Priest over the house of God, let us hold fast the confession of our hope without wavering, For He who promised is faithful. Hebrews 10:21,23

Seeing then that we have a great High Priest who has passed through the heavens, Jesus the Son of God, let us hold fast our confession Hebrews 4:14

3.   Profit in the way you should go

Thus says the Lord your redeemer, The Holy One of Israel I am the Lord your God, who teaches you to profit who leads you by the way you should go Isa. 48:17

Building Your Legacy

Making It Intentional

He commanded our ancestors to teach them to their children, so the next generation might know them--even the children not yet born--and they in turn will teach their own children. —Psalm 78:5

Mary from the moment she appears in Scripture, we see her yielding to the Spirit of God. In contrast her cousin's husband Zacharias displayed unbelief, then became dumb for nine months, after he questioned the angel messenger Gabriel.

When Mary received her news, she respectfully asked a question. But went on to say, "May it be unto me Lord as you have said." Here are seven scriptures that will support your intention to live a life of blessing and legacy.

1. **We will not hide these truths from our children;** we will tell the next generation about the glorious deeds of the LORD, about his power and his mighty wonders. Psalm 78:4
2. **Tell your children about it in the years to come,** and let your children tell their children. Pass the story down from generation to generation. Joel 1:3
3. **Let each generation tell its children** of your mighty acts; let them proclaim your power. Psalm 145:4
4. Now that I am old and gray, do not abandon me, O God. **Let me proclaim your power to this new generation,** your mighty miracles to all who come after me. Psalm 71:18
5. **I am reminded of your sincere faith,** which first lived in your grandmother Lois and in your mother Eunice and, I am persuaded, now lives in you also. 2 Timothy 1:5
6. **I am writing to Timothy, my true son in the faith.** May God the Father and Christ Jesus our Lord give you grace, mercy, and peace. 1 Timothy 1:2

7. **He commanded our ancestors to teach them to their children,** so the next generation might know them--even the children not yet born--and they in turn will teach their own children. So each generation should set its hope anew on God, not forgetting his glorious miracles and obeying his commands. Then they will not be like their ancestors--stubborn, rebellious, and unfaithful, refusing to give their hearts to God. Psalm 78:5-8

Like our featured mother Mary, we can choose intentionally to live legacy all the time, that is with the next generation in mind with all we do.

Strengthening Your Legacy

8 Little Steps To MEDITATE On God's Word

But Mary treasuring all these things in her heart and meditating on them. — Luke 2:19

I believe one of the secrets of Mary living the kind of life she lived in humility and ultimately a *yielded vessel* is because she treasured and pondered on the things of God. Remember in the FIGHT section of this book, God gave Joshua this principle of success to be victorious in life, in general, but especially with possessing the occupied (with giants) Promised Land.

Meditation, many times, covers only two or three verses of Scripture at a time. To get started, read a verse, several times. Roll it over in your mind; be quiet and listen to God for twenty or thirty minutes. Here's a little eight step analogy called M.E.D.I.T.A.T.E. to help you know how to meditate on God's word.

- **Muse** on the integrity of God's word.
- **Envision** yourself as God sees you.
- **Dwell** on how this word from the Lord changes your situation.
- **Invite** the Holy Spirit to make God's word a reality in your heart.
- **Think** about, carefully, personalize this word of God to your life.
- **Agree** with what God's word says about you.
- **Talk** about the word of God with a friend.

- **Engross** yourself in a specific revelation from the word of God.

To cement the word of God, you are meditating on, personalize it into a prayer or affirmation. Then speak it seven to ten times in the morning and seven to ten times in the evening. The word will then take root in your mind and heart. It will begin to bud; first the bud then the blade, then the leaf and so on.

You know similar to how you see a plant progress in the natural. As the word of God is deposited in your heart, it will begin to bear fruit. It will grow and change what needs changing. The Holy Spirit may give you a next step scripture to meditate on, within the same topic.

❧

A Legacy Of Prayer

10 Point Prayer Of Release

Stop forming inappropriate relationships with unbelievers. Can right and wrong be partners? Can light have anything in common with darkness? Can Christ agree with the devil? Can a believer share life with an unbeliever? — 2 Corinthians 6:14,15

Sometimes our parents and/or our ancestors have broken covenant with God in ways that we know nothing about. Yet, many times the effects of it will reach throughout the generations. At least, until someone in the family through revelation from God breaks the evil cycle.

Before praying the Prayer Of Release below, you should familiarize yourself with four main areas that many overlook. Through lack of knowledge or unbelief, they mistakenly think it has nothing to do with the effects of the curse in their life and ultimately the blessing of God. So, any of the Scripture references take the time to read the verses for yourself.

It builds your faith for a miraculous release. And there's a reason, I source everything. It's so you can know for yourself. You don't have to and nor should you depend on everything I say at face value.

1. **Repent - Revoke – Replace.**

The cycle repeats itself, from generation to generation at least until someone in the family through revelation from God breaks the evil cycle. They repent, revoke and replace evil actions with good, turning from sin and renewing the family's covenant with God. What about psychics, Horoscopes, and New Age? Simply said, the Bible says rebellion is as witchcraft. Deuteronomy 18: 10-13

2. **Cancel every evil word spoken against** your family, business, your ministry and ability to prosper.

Often people make negative comments, even slanderous remarks that carry evil energy with it. The devil seeks to carry out those words. We can pray and cancel any evil spoken words against our family or business. The word of God says, "No weapon formed against you will prosper. Every evil spoken word, you will rise up and refute it."

3. **Cancel negative confessions about yourself.**

First, we must recognize that we have made a negative confession about ourselves and we must repent of it. Second, we revoke it - that is, unsay or cancel it. Third, we must replace our previous wrong confession with the right one.

4. **After all this, acknowledge Christ** and pray the prayer of release. You may have prayed the prayer separately above. It's o.k. to pray it again in the full prayer of release below. I separated it for teaching and easy explanation.

10 Point Prayer of Release

1. Lord Jesus Christ, I believe that You are the Son of God and the only way to God; and that you died on the cross for my sins and rose again from the dead.

2. I give up all my rebellion (known and unknown) and all my sin and I submit myself to you as my Lord.

3. I confess all my sins before you and ask for your forgiveness, especially for any sins that may have exposed us to a curse.

4. I make a decision of my will; I forgive all who have harmed me or wronged me -- just as I want God to forgive me. In particular, I forgive [name the person or persons]

5. In Jesus Name, I release myself from every evil inheritance from my father and mother. I renounce the occult, new age, physic involvement. I release myself from every curse related to this sin. I am neither barren or unfruitful.

6. In Jesus name, we release our self from every curse spoken against our business and household. I cancel every evil word spoken against me personally, my business, my ministry, my house, my home, my life and property.

7. I Renounce all contact with anything occult or satanic. If I have any 'contact objects' I commit myself to destroy them. I cancel all Satan's claims against me. In 2 Corinthians 6:14-15 The Apostle Paul stresses the necessity of a complete break with Satan's kingdom. What fellowship can light have with darkness?

8. I let go all unholy connections and relationships. What harmony is there between Christ and Belial (Satan) In verse 17 there's a direct charge from the Lord himself. 'Therefore, come out from among them and be separate, says the Lord.'

9. Lord Jesus, I believe that on the cross, you took on yourself every curse that could ever come upon me or against me. So, I ask you now to release me from every curse over my life - in your name, Lord Jesus Christ.

10. By faith, I now receive my release and I thank you for it. Lord, I now open myself to your blessing in every way, you want to impart it to me. Holy Spirit, I open my heart and mind to You. Reveal to us the blessings that Jesus has obtained for me and how I may receive them.

Now, continue to thank the Lord for all he has done for you through the days, weeks and months to come. To make sure I give due credit of another author's work, the 10 Point Prayer of Release was inspired by Derek Prince's book, Blessing or Curse.

Legacy Snippet

5 Simple Steps To Write A Word Inspired Manifesto

Tell your children about it in the years to come, and let your children tell their children. Pass the story down from generation to generation. —Joel 1:3

Simply put, a manifesto is a statement of ideas and intentions. The difference between a plain manifesto and a Word inspired manifesto is the power of God's word. So, make sure you put plenty of personalized scripture in your document.

The actual word manifesto comes from Latin manifestus; to clearly reveal, to make known. It is rooted from the word manifest; something clear or obvious to the eye; readily perceived by the eye; evident, obvious, apparent — such as a manifest error.

Seth Godin http://sethgodin.typepad.com/ published his manifesto entitled, "Brainwashed: Seven Ways to Reinvent Yourself," which exposes myths many people have lived by for years. A Jesus Manifesto: Restoring the Supremacy and Sovereignty of Jesus Christ by Leonard Sweet and Frank Viola is a Christian manifesto on the Amazon's top 10 bestseller list. Their website is http://www.thejesusmanifesto.com/

How To Write Your Own Manifesto

Your story is important. It's worth being heard. How can I say that and mean it? In Christ, everyone has a story to tell. And not just everybody and anybody, YOU have a story that will make the world a better place.

Usually, a manifesto is personal. Even, an organization's manifesto written by whomever is at the helm comes out personal.

It is a powerful way of expressing what's important to you at your core. It usually has your goals, strategies, wish list, dreams and beliefs—your statement of faith. Writing a manifesto will help you focus on what's really important to you. So, let's hop to it.

1. Look for inspiration.

Read some other manifestos. I linked to Seth Godin and the Jesus Manifesto. Corbett Barr wrote this brilliant "Expert Enough" http://expertenough.com manifesto to remind every one of us of our own brilliance. There are plenty to choose from. Also, see the WOW! Women Manifesto in the study guide section of this book or visit the WOW! Women website for a free printable copy of the WOW! Women of Legacy Study Guide and lots of other resources designed to inspire you to become the WOW! Women, God has called us to become.

2. Make Notes.

Your manifesto should have three basic components: beliefs, goals, and wisdom. Get a notepad and write "I believe..." at the top of a blank page, then think of five or ten ways to finish the statement.

On the next page, write "I want to..." and fill in the blanks with ways that you would change the world. Finally, write "I know this to be true..." and record words of wisdom. These can be things you've learned from your own experience, wisdom passed down from your parents and family, inspirational quotes or scripture verses.

3. Figure out what's important to you.

- What are your most beloved core beliefs?
- What are your goals and dreams?
- What are you willing to do, even sacrifice, to achieve them?
- What is your main motivation to do what you do?
- What makes you tick?
- What do you want your legacy to be?

4. Get what's inside your heart out.

Write down all the answers you can think of to the questions. No one counting how many. Just empty your heart.

Be specific with what you write. No worries about who's going to see it and what they might think. Remember, it's YOUR manifesto.

5. Tweak it until it's the way you want it.

Seek to use words everyone will understand, about seventh grade level. Be brief. Brevity creates clarity. If you rambled while you dumped, it all out. Cut the rambling. Be more concise. Make it readable. Remove all duplicates and redundancy.

Okay, it's your turn! Are you ready to write your manifesto?

Summing It All Up

I was encouraged to know we can and should live a life of legacy, intentionally. Passing the torch of life can be tricky. But not if we depend on God for our posterity. It is his aim and good pleasure for us to pass our prepared legacy of blessing to the next generation.

It took me the longest to realize the importance and power in meditating God's word. I grew faster with leaps and bounds, after I implemented it in my life. Even so, one of my biggest blocks was learning how to meditate. I, finally got the hang of it. So, I was happy when the Holy Spirit gave me the little analogy MEDITATE to help you. So, you don't have to delay with putting godly meditation in place in your life.

The 10 Point Prayer Of Release is a huge booster for releasing your life from the generational curses that bind and seek to hinder us in our blessed life. As we discussed earlier in the book, many times, they are passed down without us even knowing. Now through the word of God and the Holy Spirit's guidance, you can break any cycles of sin and the bondage it brings to oppress your family.

Legacy Challenge 6

Prepare a journal of your life's lessons five to ten. You know the things your mother and grandmother told you that you want to pass to your children. Consider what you learned or was reminded of in this book. Pass those principles along, as well. Get another copy of this book or all three WOW! Women books. Find someone at least one generation removed from yours and give it to them. It can be your daughter, a niece, or a younger cousin. Put a note inside one of the books explaining the reason you did this. Ask them to do the same, when they grow up.

Chapter Seven

Summary

*A*re you designing your life as a torch? With your eye on the next generation, you've decided, no matter what, you want to live your life well as an example. There's good news! You can live a life of legacy.

God is a god of the generations. He is the same yesterday, today and forever. Through God's plan, our generation prepares and passes the torch to the next. Inside this book series, my mission was to help you discover seven steps to prepare and live your life as a legacy:

Chapter One Leaving A Legacy brought focus to each of us becoming a shining star? A little girl was born in a time of turmoil for Israel. She was an orphan with no future and no destiny. Or so it seemed, what happened next could have changed her future and the generations to come. But Esther learned a secret that brought salvation to her nation with an unexpected upset of her enemies' plans, so powerful that it echoes through the centuries.

Esther embraced her preparation season and followed the instructions from her mentors to the letter. It worked and she was ready for her Kairos season. She even discovered the real reason for her journey, to save a people. She used every ounce of her skill, discernment, wisdom, knowledge and all that had prepared her for such-a-time-as-this moment.

She stepped out in faith, prayed, fasted and received miraculous strategy to war against the evil intent of Israel's foes. Yet none of it would have done any good, if she hadn't taken the courage to act. Now it's your turn. Get started building your legacy by living it right now.

Through the generations, we take example from a woman who rose to stardom, even royalty from the meager beginnings of an orphan.

After reading *Chapter Two Tapping Into Your Inner Queen*, I hope your inner queen has emerged? Whether she has or not, no worries. You may have discovered by now; our inner game takes time to develop. So, keep tapping into your inner queen until she shines forth, fiercely.

I was inspired by Queen of Sheba's thirst for wisdom and knowledge. I was thrilled to discover queens are smart and they seek out new ideas and opportunities. No need to wait for your ship to come in. You can hire a shuttle boat and sail out to the ship.

Either way, now is the time. Look what happened for Queen of Sheba and others like her, including me. Her thirst for knowledge led her to journey across the known world to an education fit for a queen. Eventually, it served as an example to women all over the world in many languages and worlds. Jesus used her as example to say her drive to pursue wisdom and knowledge from across the known world will put those with lazy faith to shame?

She stepped out and changed her nation for the better. You know the story by now. God did it for her. He's doing it for me. And he will do it for you.

Chapter Three Breaking The Generational Curse brought a somberness to my mind and heart but clarity. Did you get started breaking generational curses and sealing the blessing in your life? I re-discovered this topic is heavy but needful. Because of lack of knowledge, like me, you may have a tide of wrong words to turn. Be patient with waiting for the Lord to act. It takes time to change the tide. Keep working out your salvation, meditating the word of God, speaking the word of God and agreeing with God. It will change.

Again, I was somber to realize Queen Jezebel had a strong gift of influence, as most women do. Yet, her strong power to influence went beyond normal; it overflowed into an evil spirit of control, never taking no as an answer. I hope you remember, as I did, we women all have a gift of influence and power in our words to be responsible for, to a holy God.

History records Queen J's gifts and talents were extraordinary but for evil. What a different story we could be writing, if she had only learned how to stir up her husband and children to love God and good works. Remember, we are writing our own story with words. I encourage you to write it well. For it surely will be told.

With man it's impossible but with God all things are possible! rang in my heart and mind, after reading *Chapter Four Defeating The Giants Of Your Generation.* So, are you ready to defeat the giants of your generation? Two women faced with a hard decision at the crossroads of life. Either way, their destinies would be changed.

One chose to go back and the other chose to go forward. They both grew to become historic matriarchs in the lives of their family and the people of God. Through God's sovereignty the results resound through the centuries to now. What did they use to change their destiny, their future and the lives of others forever? They used the secret power of choice to pivot their destiny and leave a legacy, like no other.

I realized afresh giants can be scary, real or perceived. So, I'm glad we have a God that loves us. He has sent angels to minister to and help us. We can know, he fights for us; the battle is not ours but his. So, any giant screaming obscenities to your generation is a defeated foe. Somberly, I realized it doesn't mean it's not dangerous. Most battles are dangerous. For we must fight God's way; get his instructions and depend on him to defeat the giants of our generations.

Furthermore, we thank God that all Scripture is God-breathed and inspired by him. It is useful for instruction and setting a great pattern that we can follow. Through the choice of hope Ruth made and the heart of repentance and obedience of her great-grandson King David, we are inspired to overcome the giants in our generation. We can take up the five smooth stones of revelation and throw the Rock of Ages and hit our giant enemy right between the eyes. Run up with the sword of the Spirit and chop his head off. Then shout for the victory is ours, even to our children's children! Hallelujah!

Chapter Five Passing The Torch Of Legacy brought front and center that most people don't have the mindset of legacy. So, the question comes again, are you preparing a baton to pass to the next generation yet? I get a happy thought whenever I think about the fact that we serve a God that's generational in thinking. Throughout the Bible, he mentions several generations in passing information and most importantly making covenant.

It's the same way with you and me. The promises of God are for us and our children. A person can be a noted successful person to build a dynasty, an empire in their lifetime. We discovered it becomes really extraordinary when you find a person that has generational vision.

It was encouraging to study Lois and Eunice who were commended for their personal faith in the New Testament. With God's help, they rose above the rest, in their personal faith and preparing their life as a legacy to pass.

Catching the Apostle's attention, they became famous for raising the godly young man, Timothy in the midst of an ungodly society. They prepared a torch of legacy for the generations to come. He turned out to be the Apostle Paul's most trusted companion, disciple and beloved son of the gospel.

Chapter Six Living The Legacy hopefully prepared your heart to apply God's word. I was encouraged to know we can and should live a life of legacy, intentionally. Passing the torch of life can be tricky. But not if we depend on God for our posterity. It is his aim and good pleasure for us to pass our prepared legacy of blessing to the next generation.

It took me the longest to realize the importance and power in meditating God's word. I grew faster with leaps and bounds, after I implemented it in my life. One of my blocks was learning how to meditate. So, I was happy when the Holy Spirit gave me the little analogy MEDITATE to help you.

The Prayer Of Release was a huge booster for releasing your life from the generational curse that binds and seeks to hinder us in our blessed life. As we discussed earlier in the book, many times, they are passed down without us even knowing. Now, through the power of Christ, the word of God and the Holy Spirit's guidance, you can break any cycles of sin and bondage oppressing your family.

Again, it's your turn. Who are you mentoring and pouring into? If not already, get started praying about someone today. Start living your life as a legacy.

While writing this book, I discovered afresh, Father God wants the same for each generation. God said to Moses, "I AM WHO I AM. God, furthermore, said to Moses, "Thus you shall say to the sons of Israel, 'The LORD, the God of your fathers, the God of Abraham, the God of Isaac, and the God of Jacob, has sent me to you.' This is My name forever, and this is My memorial-name to all generations. Exodus 3:14,15 So, it is with each generation; he is the I AM forever and to all the generations.

Furthermore, Father God has put in each of us a blueprint, the thoughts, plans and hope for a bright future. I have designed the WOW! Women message to hopefully position you to receive God's plans to satisfy that longing. Start your journey today using the seven lessons in everything you do and experience the joy of leaving a legacy of a life well-lived.

Legacy Challenge 7

It's God's way that we continue in learning little by little. He knows we are frail creatures. So, as not to overwhelm us He gives it to us step by step. "He tells us everything over and over--one line at a time, one line at a time, a little here, and a little there!" —Isaiah 28:10 Write below your favorite concept or scripture from the WOW! Women of Legacy book. Meditate on it this week or as long as you want.

Action Guides

Small Group Study Guide

1. Legacy Challenges 1–7
2. 7 Star Power Affirmations
3. Affirmations Fit For A Queen
4. 8 Little Steps To MEDITATE On God's Word
5. 10 Point Prayer Of Release
6. 5 Simple Steps To Write A Word Inspired Manifesto
7. WOW! Women Manifesto

Visit the WOW! Women website for free printable study guide for this book and the other two books of the WOW! Women series: http://www.wowontheweb.com

1.) Legacy Challenges 1–7

Legacy Challenge 1

Log in at http://wowotheweb.com and pick up your copy of the WOW! Women of Legacy's crown logo and put it on your website and blog. Continue in your QUEEN training and reign as you go.

_____

_____

_____

_____

_____

_____

_____

Legacy Challenge 2

Create a manifesto of the affirmations and confessions from the last two chapters. Start with the Affirmations Fit For A Queen section. Need more go to Chapter One in the YOU Are A Shining Star section. Also, if not already visit Earma at the WOW! Women website for additional scripture based affirmations. http://www.wowontheweb.com

_____
_____
_____
_____
_____
_____
_____
_____

Legacy Challenge 3

Applying the word of God: Go on a word fast. For example, start a two-day fast of no complaints. If you even start a complaint, you must replace it with a compliment or a grateful statement about the same thing. To hold yourself accountable, tell a friend what you are doing or make a post on Facebook. Next time, do it for a week. Let us know at http://wowontheweb.com under testimonials how it went.

_____
_____
_____
_____
_____
_____
_____
_____

Legacy Challenge 4

Write down the three scriptures that stood out to you the most, from the '11 Ways To Reverence God More and More section. Meditate on them this week or as long you want. Write down what God speaks to you about them.

_____

_____

_____

_____

_____

_____

_____

_____

Legacy Challenge 5

Talk to someone about heaven. Tell them the good news about heaven, whether it's someone who's Christian relative just died. Or choose someone you know that needs to hear the message of Christ and the hope of heaven. Make a few notes below or in your journal about what you would say.

_____

_____

_____

_____

_____

_____

_____

_____

Legacy Challenge 6

Prepare a journal of your life's lessons five to ten. You know the things your mother and grandmother told you that you want to pass to your children. Consider what you learned or was reminded of in this book. Pass those principles along, as well. Get another copy of this book or all three books. Find someone at least one generation removed from yours and give it to them. It can be your daughter, a niece, or a younger cousin. Put a note inside one of the books explaining the reason you did this. Ask them to do the same, when they grow up.

_____

_____

_____

_____

_____

_____

_____

_____

Legacy Challenge 7

It's God's way that we learn a little by little. He knows we are frail creatures. So, as not to overwhelm us He gives it to us step by step. "He tells us everything over and over--one line at a time, one line at a time, a little here, and a little there!" —Isaiah 28:10 Write below your favorite concept or scripture from the WOW! Women of Legacy book. Meditate on it this week or as long as you want.

_____

_____

_____

_____

_____

_____

_____

_____

Other Action Guides

2.) 7 Star Power Affirmations: Memorize Meditate Speak

Now that we know we are called to be stars for Jesus, here are six confessions to memorize, meditate, and speak over yourself and others in your life.

- **I am a shining star for Jesus.** May any fame I attain reflect Christ to a dark world. "So that no one can criticize you. Live clean, innocent lives as children of God, shining like bright stars in a world full of crooked and perverse people." —Philippians 2:15
- **I radiate light wherever I go.** "You are the light of the world. A town built on a hill cannot be hidden." —Matthew 5:14
- **I shine like a firework in the night.** "Then you will shine among them like stars in the sky." —Philippians 2:15
- **I am a daughter of Light.** "You are all children of the light and children of the day. We do not belong to the night or to the darkness." —1 Thessalonians 5:5
- **I am the salt of the earth.** "You are the salt of the earth." —Matthew 5:13
- **I am a vessel of His Light.** "For God, who said, "Let light shine out of darkness," made his light shine in our hearts to give us the light of the knowledge of God's glory displayed in the face of Christ." —2 Corinthians 4:6
- **Beams and light and joy exude from within me.** "Light shines on the godly, and joy on those whose hearts are right." —Psalm 97:11

After you embrace your self-worth, your beauty and joy in Christ, you have the fearlessness and fierceness to step into your destiny and reign... For more affirmations and declarations, visit http://wowontheweb.com for the WOW! Women Manifesto and how to create your own manifesto.

3.) Affirmations Fit For A Queen

Develop your Christ gift. Most of what God gives comes in seed form. I know there are exceptions, brilliant genius that are born with a ten talent gift. But most of us, have to work at it. We start out with normal proficiency. You doing what we can, when we can. Then, if we keep developing, we come to an expert status. We don't let anything stop us. We keep going and going, until we arrive at genius level. For now, here are some affirmations Fit For A Queen.

- **I am a victor.**

"No, in all these things we are more than conquerors through him who loved us." Romans 8:37

- **I have a heavenly calling.**

"Therefore, holy brothers and sisters, who share in the heavenly calling, fix your thoughts on Jesus, whom we acknowledge as our apostle and high priest." Hebrews 3:1

- **I have royalty in my veins and lead with integrity.**

"But you are a chosen people, a royal priesthood, a holy nation, God's special possession, that you may declare the praises of him who called you out of darkness into his wonderful light." 1 Peter 2:9

- **I am designed for good works.**

"For we are God's handiwork, created in Christ Jesus to do good works, which God prepared in advance for us to do." Ephesians 2:10

- **I am a co-heir with Christ.**

"Now if we are children, then we are heirs- heirs of God and co-heirs with Christ. If indeed we share in His sufferings in order that we may also share with His glory." Romans 8:17

- **I am chosen and called by God to produce fruit.**

"You did not choose me, but I chose you and appointed you so that you might go and bear fruit—fruit that will last—and so that whatever you ask in my name the Father will give you." John 15:16

Now, speak the bolded declarations out loud to yourself. The power of life and death is in the tongue, so it is vital that you only allow the Truth to come out of your mouth. It could be the difference in an amazing life or a disappointing one. (Proverbs 18:21)

4.)   8 Little Steps To MEDITATE On God's Word

Meditation, many times, covers only two or three verses of Scripture. Read a verse, several times. Roll it over in your mind; be quiet and listen to God for twenty or thirty minutes. Here's a little eight step analogy called M.E.D.I.T.A.T.E. to help you know how to meditate on God's word.

Muse on the integrity of God's word.

Envision yourself as God sees you.

Dwell on how this word from the Lord changes your situation.

Invite the Holy Spirit to make God's word a reality in your heart.

Think about, carefully, personalize this word of God to your life.

Agree with what God's word says about you.

Talk about the word of God with a friend.

Engross yourself in a specific revelation from the word of God.

To cement the word of God, you are meditating on, personalize it into a prayer or affirmation. Then speak it ten times in the morning and ten times in the evening. The word will then take root in your mind and heart. It will begin to bud; first the bud then the blade, then the leaf and so on. You know similar to how you see a plant progress in the natural. As the word of God is deposited in your heart, it will begin to bear fruit. It will grow and change what needs changing. The Holy Spirit may give you a next step scripture to meditate on, within the same topic.

5.)   10 Point Prayer Of Release

Breaking Any Generational Curse And Sealing The Blessing

Before praying the *Prayer Of Release* below, you should familiarize yourself with four main areas that many overlook. Through lack of knowledge or unbelief, they mistakenly think it has nothing to do with the effects of the curse in their life and ultimately the blessing of God.

So, any of the Scripture references take the time to read the verses for yourself. It builds your faith for a miraculous release. And there's a reason, I source everything. It's so you can know for yourself. You don't have to and nor should you depend on everything I say at face value.

Pre-Prayer #1   Repent - Revoke - Replace

Sometimes our parents and/or our ancestors have broken covenant with God in ways that we know nothing about. Yet, many times the effects of it will reach throughout the generations. At least, until someone in the family through revelation from God breaks the evil cycle. They repent, turn from sin and renew the family's covenant with God. What about psychics, Horoscopes, and New Age? Rebellion is as witchcraft. —Deuteronomy 18: 10-13

Prayer: In Jesus Name, I release myself from every evil inheritance from my father and mother. I renounce the occult, new age, physic involvement. I release myself from every curse related to this sin. I am neither barren or unfruitful.

Pre-Prayer #2   Cancel every evil word spoken against your business, your ministry and ability to prosper.

Often people make negative comments, even slanderous remarks that carry evil energy with it. The devil seeks to carry out those words. We can pray and cancel any evil spoken words against our family or business. The word of God says, "No weapon formed against you will prosper. Every evil spoken word, you will rise up and refute it."

Prayer: In Jesus name, we release our self from every curse spoken against our business and household.

Pre-Prayer #3   Cancel negative confessions about yourself.

First, we must recognize that we have made a negative confession about ourselves and we must repent of it. Second, we revoke it – that is, unsay or cancel it. Third, we must replace our previous wrong confession with the right one.

Pre-Prayer #4   Then, Acknowledge Christ and pray the prayer of release.

You may have prayed the prayer separately above. It's o.k. to pray it again in the full prayer of release below. I separated it for teaching and easy explanation.

10 Point Prayer of Release

1.   Lord Jesus Christ, I believe that You are the Son of God and the only way to God; and that you died on the cross for my sins and rose again from the dead.

2.   I give up all my rebellion (known and unknown) and all my sin and I submit myself to you as my Lord.

3.   I confess all my sins before you and ask for your forgiveness, especially for any sins that may have exposed us to a curse.

4.   I make a decision of my will; I forgive all who have harmed me or wronged me -- just as I want God to forgive me. In particular, I forgive [name the person or persons]

5.   In Jesus Name, I release myself from every evil inheritance from my father and mother. I renounce the occult, new age, physic involvement. I release myself from every curse related to this sin. I am neither barren or unfruitful.

6.   In Jesus name, we release our self from every curse spoken against our business and household. I cancel every evil word spoken against me personally, my business, my ministry, my house, my home, my life and property.

7.   I Renounce all contact with anything occult or satanic. If I have any 'contact objects' I commit myself to destroy them. I cancel all Satan's claims against me. In 2 Corinthians 6:14-15 The Apostle Paul stresses the necessity of a complete break with Satan's kingdom. What fellowship can light have with darkness?

8.   I let go all unholy connections and relationships. What harmony is there between Christ and Belial (Satan) In verse 17 there's a direct charge from the Lord himself. 'Therefore, come out from among them and be separate, says the Lord.'

9.   Lord Jesus, I believe that on the cross, you took on yourself every curse that could ever come upon me or against me. So, I ask you now to release me from every curse over my life – in your name, Lord Jesus Christ.

10. By faith, I now receive my release and I thank you for it. Lord, I now open myself to your blessing in every way, you want to impart it to me. Holy Spirit, I open my heart and mind to You. Reveal to us the blessings that Jesus has obtained for me and how I may receive them.

Now, continue to thank the Lord for all he has done for you through the days, weeks and months to come.

6.)   5 Simple Steps To Write A Word Inspired Manifesto

Tell your children about it in the years to come, and let your children tell their children. Pass the story down from generation to generation. -Joel 1:3

Simply put, a manifesto is a statement of ideas and intentions. The difference between a plain manifesto and a Word inspired manifesto is the power of God's word. So, make sure you put plenty of personalized scripture in your document.

The actual word manifesto comes from Latin manifestus; to clearly reveal, to make known. It is rooted from the word manifest; something clear or obvious to the eye; readily perceived by the eye; evident, obvious, apparent — such as a manifest error.

Seth Godin http://sethgodin.typepad.com/ published his manifesto entitled, "Brainwashed: Seven Ways to Reinvent Yourself," which exposes myths many people have lived by for years. A Jesus Manifesto: Restoring the Supremacy and Sovereignty of Jesus Christ by Leonard Sweet and Frank Viola is a Christian manifesto on the Amazon's top 10 bestseller list. Their website is http://www.thejesusmanifesto.com/

How To Write Your Own Manifesto

Your story is important. It's worth being heard. How can I say that and mean it? In Christ, everyone has a story to tell. And not just everybody and anybody, YOU have a story that will make the world a better place.

Usually, a manifesto is personal. Even, an organization's manifesto written by whomever is at the helm comes out personal.

It is a powerful way of expressing what's important to you at your core. It usually has your goals, strategies, wish list, dreams and beliefs—your statement of faith. Writing a manifesto will help you focus on what's really important to you. So, let's hop to it.

Step 1. Look for inspiration.

Read some other manifestos. I linked to Seth Godin and the Jesus Manifesto. Corbett Barr wrote this brilliant "Expert Enough" http://expertenough.com manifesto to remind every one of us of our own brilliance. There are plenty to choose from. Also, see the WOW! Women Manifesto in the study guide section of this book or visit the WOW! Women website for a free printable copy of the WOW! Women of Legacy Study Guide and lots of other resources designed to inspire you to become the WOW! Women, God has called us to become.

Step 2. Make Notes.

Your manifesto should have three basic components: beliefs, goals, and wisdom. Get a notepad and write "I believe..." at the top of a blank page, then think of five or ten ways to finish the statement. On the next page, write "I want to..." and fill in the blanks with ways that you would change the world. Finally, write "I know this to be true..." and record words of wisdom. These can be things you've learned from your own experience, wisdom passed down from your parents and family, inspirational quotes or scripture verses.

Step 3. Figure out what's important to you.

- What are your most beloved core beliefs?
- What are your goals and dreams?
- What are you willing to do, even sacrifice, to achieve them?
- What is your main motivation to do what you do?
- What makes you tick?
- What do you want your legacy to be?

Step 4. Get what's inside your heart out.

Write down all the answers you can think of to the questions. No one counting how many. Just empty your heart.

Be specific with what you write. No worries about who's going to see it and what they might think. Remember, it's YOUR manifesto.

Step 5. Tweak it until it's the way you want it.

Seek to use words everyone will understand, about seventh grade level. Be brief. Brevity creates clarity. If you rambled while you dumped, it all out. Cut the rambling. Be more concise. Make it readable. Remove all duplicates and redundancy.

Okay, it's your turn! Are you ready to write your manifesto?

7.) WOW! WOMEN MANIFESTO

We are passionate about God's creation WOMAN and we want the world to know it. Loving deeply, listening more and caring also top the list of things we courageously live. Get to know our WOW! Women manifesto and learn a little more about what lights our fire, maybe yours too.

WOMEN GROW UP WITH SO MANY WRONG IDEAS ABOUT WHO WE SHOULD BE--WHAT WE SHOULD LOOK LIKE, WHAT WE SHOULD DO AND WHAT OUR LIVES SHOULD BE LIKE.

Sometimes they come from well-meaning people, evil people or simply misguided thoughts about ourselves.

We spend the early part of our lives cowing down, conforming, letting it go, compromising, fitting in or backing back. When we give it a try expressing ourselves fully with moving beyond what's expected we're often corrected...chastised...even crushed.

WE'RE TOLD WE'RE TOO MUCH, TOO LOUD, TOO EXPRESSIVE, TOO BIG.

So we

- pull back and
- rein it in.
- We tuck ourselves in.
- We quieten our voices.
- We don't rock the boat, so no one gets upset.
- Our world and our lives become smaller.

BUT THEN WE WAKE UP, MOVE FORWARD, STEP UP

WE SAY, 'ENOUGH! I WILL NOT LIVE SOMEONE ELSE'S VISION OF MY LIFE!'

I will now be what I should've been yesterday, today and forever...

I am the heroine in my own story. **Just Be**

God made us free day by day, more free than we ever thought we could be.

SOMETHING INSIDE LEAPS AGAIN.

WE'RE FIERCE! WE'RE FREE!

WE'RE HOLY! WE'RE GOD'S CHOSEN

no longer do we:

APOLOGIZE FOR WHO WE ARE

LET OTHERS DEFINE US

BETRAY OURSELVES

NOW--100% OF THE TIME, WE

STEP UP

STAND OUT

CELEBRATE OUR WOMANHOOD NOW

IT'S YOUR TIME!

- Time to be FAITHFUL and DARING and BOLD
- Time to DREAM BIG and TAKE ACTION
- Time to Say YES More To GOD, Life And Family
- Time to take RISKS, make MISTAKES, EXPERIMENT MORE and GROW
- Time to OWN YOUR POWER AND FORGE YOUR FAITH
- Time to WALK your PATH and DESTINY!

Become A Shining Star!

Shining star for you to see, what your life can truly be... -Earth, Wind & Fire.

Today. Right Now. It's Your Time To SHINE!

Bibliography

o   Joyce Meyers, The Confident Woman: Start Today Living Boldly And Without Fear (Warner Faith Hachette Book Group, 2006)

o   Ann Spangler & Jean E. Syswerda, Women of the Bible, A One-Year Devotional Study of Women In Scripture (Zondervan Publishing House, 1999.)

o   Sue and Larry Richards, Every Woman In The Bible, Fully Illustrated (Thomas Nelson Publishers, 1999.)

o   Joyce Meyers, How to Succeed at Being Yourself: Finding the Confidence to Fulfill Your Destiny (Tulsa: Harrison House, 1999.)

o   J.W. Martin (Compiled by), The Spirit-Filled Woman (Lake Mary: Creation House, 1997.)

o   Elizabeth George, Beautiful in God's Eyes (Eugene: Harvest House Publishers, 1998.)

o   Elizabeth George, A Woman After God's Own Heart (Eugene: Harvest House Publishers, 1995.)

o   Laurie Beth Jones, Jesus CEO: Using Ancient Wisdom for Visionary Leadership (New York: Laurie Beth Jones, 1995.)

o   Dr. Lester Sumrall, The Names of God: God's Name Brings Hope, Healing, and Happiness (New Kensington: Whitaker House, 1996.)

o   Fred and Anna Kendall with Mary Hollingsworth, Speaking of Love: Learn the 7 Behavioral Life Languages of Highly Effective Communication (Dallas: Fred and Anna Kendall, 1995.)

o   Joni Lamb, Surrender All: Your Answer to Living with Peace, Power & Purpose (Colorado Springs: Waterbrook Press, 2008.)

o   Linda Weber, Woman of Splendor: Discovering the Four Facets of a Godly Woman (Nashville, Broadman & Holman Publishers, 1999.)

- O Carolyn Savelle, The Intensity of Your Desires, The Keys to Unlocking the Answers to Your Prayers (Crowley: Jerry Savelle Publications, 2000.)
- O Cynthia Heald, Becoming a Woman of excellence (Colorado Springs: NavPress, 2005.)
- O Cynthia Heald, Becoming a Woman of Prayer (Colorado Springs: NavPress, 2005.)
- O Derek Prince, Blessing or Curse (Choice Books, 1990.)

thank You Note

hank you for reading the WOW! Women of Legacy book. I'm so excited that all three books are officially here! Just to let you know a little bit more about me, I am a victorious ex-victim of spousal abuse. I stand upon the God-given platform of my past proclaiming the gospel of God's grace to women of any background with any struggle. I developed the WOW! Women books from a Bible study and class (WOW! Women of Worth) I, originally, wrote for battered women re-building their self-image and life in God.

It all started with Father God giving me the confidence to teach Bible study to a rowdy bunch of women maximum security inmates. Trembling with fear, I asked Father God what to say to them. He said to me, "Tell them they're WOW! Women of Worth." I taught this study for class sessions in the Dallas, Texas prison system and later in my local church.

I gave my full testimony in the first audio class of the WOW! Women of Worth Curriculum. The classes are short but power packed, about thirty to forty minutes. You can listen and download other fun resources for free. When you join the WOW! Women Global membership, you get access to all four audio classes. Join today, here at http://www.wowontheweb.com

Again, I believe the principles God gave me to think right about myself and connect with my own destiny will apply to anyone desiring to live victoriously in Christ with strong identity and purpose. Therefore, part one of the book's theme was *Women Encouraging Women to Victory and Destiny*. The chapters were designed to leave every reader with a sense of destiny that will help her fulfill her God-given purpose.

In addition, book one's study uncovered a trail of biblical truths that affirm the answers to the four classic questions of life: 'Where did I come from?' 'Who am I' 'Why am I here?' and 'Where am I going?' From the answers of those four questions, seven steps to destiny were developed. The steps threaded throughout part one of the book included a woman's worth, image, name, mission, prayer, gift and destiny.

In book two, the biblical trail continued leading God's woman to her predestination, pursuit of God's presence, preparation, passion, purpose, perseverance in prayer, and the power to fulfill her destiny. I'm thrilled to say, the journey continued with the last book of the WOW Women book series *'WOW! Women of Legacy.* I was delighted to share the revelation God gave me for tapping into our inner queen, breaking the generational curse and overcoming the giants of our generation, to name a few. It has been quite a journey, so far. If you enjoyed the books, I invite you to continue with me and teach a WOW! Women Bible Study using our curriculum and/or join us with a WOW! Women Global membership. Get the details at http://wowwomenglobal.com

The overall message was designed to inspire women with God-ordained hope and vision for a bright future. The books have inspired many with not only vision and hope for their bright future but the ability to walk with purpose and power in their destiny. With the third book, I laid out the principles to enjoy a God ordained life, but also, leave a legacy for the generations to come. So, come on, let's do God's work together.

Leaving a legacy,
Earma, 12 Book Christian Author, Founder of WOW! Women Global
http://www.wowontheweb.com

About Author

arma Brown inspires women around the world to become women of destiny, purpose, and victory through speaking engagements, her books, Bible curriculum and studies. She is author of the trilogy of WOW! Women books: *Women of Worth, Women of Destiny* and *Women of Legacy*, along with the *Armorbearer Training Series, Prayer Fulfilled Life* books and *Writing A Book God's Way* book and course. She and her husband Varn live in Dallas Texas.

What Next?

Here's two things you can do right now to get started!

1. Get a copy of one of the other WOW! Women books. I recommend starting with the first WOW! Women of Worth book, then get the WOW! Women of Destiny and WOW! Women of Legacy, in that order. Use it for your personal study and encouragement. Then teach it to your Bible Study class, book club or small group. I'm grateful to say, I've been getting good feedback.

    If you are interested in all three, join the WOW! Women Global community with an annual membership and receive a complimentary copy of all three books along with other fun resources. When you join the WOW! Women Global community, you receive each new devotional or study guide book released during that year, free and stay connected to other women on the WOW! journey.

2. Join the tribe at WOW! Women Global Membership (Now Open – Introductory Offer) http://wowwomenglobal.com

Other WOW! Women Books & Resources

WOW! Women of Worth (Book 1)

Have you feared you would never know why you are here? If so, you are not alone a Gallup poll has determined that one of people's greatest fears is to die having lived a meaningless life. With passion and grace, author Earma Brown declares there's no better place to look for answers than the Bible. She uncovers a biblical trail of seven strategies to becoming an extraordinary woman using ordinary tools. Her book *Women of Worth* will help you live a life full of meaning while understanding how to:

- o Avoid the mistakes forever caused by low self-esteem.
- o Overcome an enemy called insignificance.
- o Defeat the dream assassins sent to kill your spirit and your dreams.
- o Unlock the potential that many never tap into.
- o Gain a sense of destiny that will change your life.

The Desire for a Bright Future! "Father God has put in each of us as a seed, the desire for a bright future," explains Earma. "I have designed the book to hopefully position the reader to receive God's plans to satisfy that longing," Start your journey today using the seven strategies in everything you do and experience the joy of becoming an extraordinary woman using ordinary tools.

WOW! Women of Destiny (Book 2)

Discover Purpose that Gives You the Power to Go to Your Destiny!

Are you a woman of God's destiny and power? With passion, grace and biblical integrity, Earma Brown lays out a map to God's destiny and purpose for women. WOW! Women of Destiny book two of the WOW! Women Series is filled with insightful encouragement for women pursuing God's destiny and purpose for their lives. Inside WOW! Women of Destiny you will discover how to:

- Seek God's presence not just the gift and receive patience with the process.
- Develop a spirit of readiness for your Kairos opportunities when they come.
- Fuel your passion with your troubles. Turn the lemons of life into lemonade.
- Discover passion that points to God's purpose. Stop the passion thieves sent to douse your passion.
- Stop the destiny thieves sent to kill your dreams and receive God ordained purpose that leads to power
- Prepare a plan that leaves a legacy in women from generation to generation.

Filled with women like Candy Lightner, the *WOW! Women of Destiny* book seeks to inspire you to know and walk in your destiny. Candy was considered a normal housewife with children. So what caused her to almost single-handedly change a nation's complacent thinking about drinking while driving? Her 12-year old daughter, Cari was killed by a drunk driver. Armed with a passion to help other mothers face similar tragedies, she formed MADD (Mothers Against Drunk Driving) and in the process turned her troubles into triumphs.

Book two of the WOW Women Book Series is an inspiring celebration of women and men from modern times and history who took hold of their destiny and making a difference in their family, church, community and world.

The author's personal experiences, cemented with biblical scripture will encourage you to overcome modern day challenges in the church, in society, as well as balancing God's call to destiny through victorious home life and community.

Down to earth and inspiring, the WOW! Women of Destiny book is not only for women's groups. It is a must read for Christian men and women alike seeking to empower their wives, sisters, mothers and daughters to fulfill their passion, purpose and power, even their destiny in God's Kingdom.

For more about the WOW Women Books and other WOW! Women resources, visit Earma at the WOW! Women Shop http://wowontheweb.com/shop/

Notes

Notes

Notes

www.ingramcontent.com/pod-product-compliance
Lightning Source LLC
Chambersburg PA
CBHW030935090426
42737CB00007B/438